ABOUT THE AUTHORS

Christian family life is a special interest of Ron and Lyn Klug as teachers, writers, editors, and parents. The Klugs served a four-year term as educators at a missionary elementary and secondary school in Madagascar. Currently they are free-lance writers and editors living in Northfield, Minnesota, with their three children.

Ron is the author of two books for boys, *You Promised, Lord* and *Lord, I've Been Thinking,* and he has written another book in this series, *Bible Readings on Prayer.* Lyn is the author of *I Know I Can Trust You, Lord,* a book for girls, and *Bible Readings for Women.* Together they have written several books for children: *Jesus Comes; Jesus Loves; Jesus Lives!; Please, God;* and *Thank You, God.* They also are the editors of the popular anthologies, *The Christian Family Bedtime Reading Book* and *The Christian Family Christmas Book.*

Bible Readings
FOR
PARENTS

Bible Readings

FOR
PARENTS

·

Ron & Lyn Klug

AUGSBURG Publishing House • Minneapolis

BIBLE READINGS FOR PARENTS

Copyright © 1982 Augsburg Publishing House

Library of Congress Catalog Card No. 81-052277

International Standard Book No. 0-8066-1909-0

Scripture quotations unless otherwise noted are from the Good News Bible, Today's English Version: copyright © American Bible Society 1966, 1971, 1976. Used by permission.

Scripture quotations marked NIV are from the Holy Bible: New International Version. Copyright 1978 by the New York International Bible Society. Used by permission of Zondervan Bible Publishers.

Scripture quotations marked KJV are from The Holy Bible: King James Version.

MANUFACTURED IN THE UNITED STATES OF AMERICA

◼ PREFACE

Jesus said, "Anyone who hears these words of mine and obeys them is like a wise man who built his house on a rock" (Matt. 7:24). Especially in a time like ours, when the Christian family is threatened from so many directions, we need to live in God's Word, to receive its guidance and strength.

When our children are old enough, we will want to read the Scriptures together and to join in song and prayer. Each parent needs time for individual reflection and prayer. As parents we may also want to spend some devotional time to reflect together on God's Word and what it says for our family life. We can think together about our family needs, problems, and joys, and we can hold the family before God in prayer. To aid in prayer time for parents, we have selected some portions of Scripture that especially speak to us as parents, and we have shared some of our reflections on these words.

In our efforts to be a Christian family we feel the same pressures as you do. We often feel inadequate. We make many mistakes. We are sometimes frustrated and discouraged. We know it is easier to preach than to practice. At the same time we feel we are learning along the way, both from our own experience and from friends. These things we have tried to put into words.

You may not find brand-new ideas here. What we have to share is not something novel, but the time-tested wisdom of Scripture and Christian experience. We find that it is not so much a matter of learning new truths as it is of reminding ourselves of truths we already know. We need these reminders as much as anyone.

It is not enough, however, just to be *reminded* of God's Word. We need his grace and the power of his Spirit to learn to do his will, to internalize these truths and put them into action. To help you begin to do that, we have suggested an activity at the end of each reading. It may be a question to discuss, a memory to share, some concrete action to take.

A Christian parent is a Christian who happens to be a parent, so the themes that run through this book are the great recurring themes of the Christian life: grace, forgiveness, discipline, self-giving, reconciliation, hope, faith. Any Christian who wishes to grow as a parent can best do so by growing as a Christian. As we grow in our relationship to God through studying his Word, through worship and prayer, and through Christian fellowship, we will receive wisdom and power for change.

As we wrote this book, we were thinking of families like our own, with both parents present. We realize, of course, that there are many single-parent families. If you are a single parent reading this book, we hope that you, too, will find here some help and encouragement.

Writing this book was a good experience for us. It made us think through our own parenting and the connections between the Christian faith and our family living. We hope that as you read this book you will learn to trust the wisdom you already have as parents and that you will find here some words of comfort, of hope, and of guidance to strengthen your life together.

■ THANK GOD FOR DIFFERENCES

Rom. 12:3-8: "We are to use our different gifts in accordance with the grace that God has given us" (v. 6).

One parent may be casual and easygoing; the other, a stickler for punctuality and neatness. One may be comfortable with noise and clutter; the other needs quiet and order. One may be a model of patience; the other may have a short fuse. These differences can cause tension as parents try to work out a consistent pattern of discipline and a harmonious life-style.

But these differences are sources of peace when we allow each parent to lead from his or her strength. For example, the "neat" parent can be the one to help children keep their toys in order. The "hang loose" parent may be the one to take a group of six-year-olds to the circus or host a birthday party. The parent who is a "morning person" may be the best one to get the kids off to school; the one who can get by on less sleep may be willing to get up in the middle of the night with a crying child.

Our differences need not divide us. They can be used to complement and support one another. Neither parent has to feel guilty or inferior for not being good at everything. We can rejoice that we don't have to be and say, "Thank God for our differences!"

We thank you, Lord, for the differing gifts you have given us. Help us make the most of our uniqueness.

Make two lists: one of the mother's strengths, one of the father's. Then list how best to use these strengths within the family.

9

■ CONFORMED OR TRANSFORMED?

Rom. 12:1-2: "Do not conform yourselves to the standards of this world, but let God transform you inwardly by a complete change of your mind" (v. 2).

If a man does not keep pace with his companions, perhaps it is because he hears a different drummer. Let him step to the music which he hears, however measured or far away." So wrote Henry David Thoreau. St. Paul said it differently: "Do not conform yourselves to the standards of this world."

By "this world" Paul meant the corrupt systems of our society, the system of values apart from God. That system is always trying to press us into its mold through our contacts with people, through TV and movies, books and magazines.

We need to be alert to what we are seeing and hearing, for we are called to be a counterculture in our attitudes toward marriage and children and family life.

The alternative to being "conformed" is to be "transformed." This happens when our minds are renewed, when we fill our minds with God's truth and let it take possession of us. Through this truth God sets us free and changes us so that we become more and more like him. Then, says Paul, "you will be able to know the will of God—what is good and is pleasing to him and is perfect."

 O Holy Spirit, alert us to the pressures that are forcing us into the world's mold. Renew and transform us by the power of your truth.

In what area of your family life are you tempted to conform to the world? How can you resist these pressures?

■ HAVE YOU HUGGED YOUR KID TODAY?

1 John 4:7-12: "Let us love one another, because love comes from God" (v. 7).

Years ago doctors in orphanages were disturbed by the large numbers of children dying from unexplained causes. The children were kept in sterile surroundings and were fed well, yet as many as 80% were dying in infancy.

Finally they figured out the reason why: the children were not being touched, hugged, carried around. The children were dying from a lack of love. When they received touches of love, they prospered.

We like the bumper sticker that says, "Have you hugged your kid today?" We need to be reminded that love needs to be expressed also in physical ways.

Because of personality differences some of us may find this harder to do than others. Perhaps men more than women have been conditioned against expressing feelings of tenderness. But there are ways to express our love that are appropriate for us: a hug, a bedtime kiss, a hand on the shoulder, some gentle tousling.

God did more than give us words about love. In the person of Jesus he came to feed the hungry and to heal the sick. We can be channels for his love to our children and to one another.

Thank you, Lord, for the touch of your love. Help us to express our love to one another.

Give one another a big hug! And remember to hug your children.

■ A CHILD'S QUESTIONS

Luke 2:41-52: ". . . listening to them and asking questions" (v. 46).

It might seem extraordinary that this twelve-year-old boy should be found among the religious teachers, amazing them with his insights and questions. Yet we are continually amazed by the questions even three- or four-year-olds ask: "Where is God?" "What happens to you when you die?" "Will God always take care of us?" A child's questions, yet they have puzzled the greatest minds of the ages.

If you're like us, you're often baffled by questions like these. You may not be sure of the answers, or you may not know how to explain such profound matters to a child. But we can encourage the questions, not only for our children's sake but for our own, as spurs to our own thinking and learning. We can answer honestly, sharing what we actually believe. And if the honest answer is, "I don't know," we can say that. We don't have to know all the answers, but we can assure our children that we too are thinking about these important questions.

As we share the light we have, our own insights will increase. Then we will have more to give our children, and they too will grow "both in body and in wisdom, gaining favor with God and men."

Lord of love, help us to listen to our children's questions. By the wisdom of your Holy Spirit help us grow together with them.

Recall incidents when your children asked some difficult religious questions. How did you answer them?

■ DON'T BUG ME!

Eph. 6:4: "Parents, do not treat your children in such a way as to make them angry."

A neighbor was walking down the street with his five-year-old daughter in tow, lecturing her at length, making the same point over and over. Finally the little girl blurted out, "Daddy, don't keep on saying that! Don't keep on saying it!"

Lecturing, nagging, and overcorrecting are some ways we can make our children angry. We can also do it by calling them names like "Stupid" or "Crybaby" or "Clumsy." We can do it by teasing or humiliating them in front of others. We can do it by ignoring them when they need to talk to us. We can do it by being unrealistic in our expectations of them.

Paul says the alternative to making our children angry isn't letting them do whatever they want. "Instead," says Paul, "raise them with Christian discipline and instruction." Christian discipline does not mean punishment, but "discipling" or teaching. We do this in the spirit of Christ if we are consistent, if we are considerate of the feelings of our children, if we discipline them whenever possible away from other people. In this way, we will not only be disciplining them, but we will be showing them the love which Christ has shown us.

Heavenly Father, give us understanding and patience so that we do not provoke our children to anger. Guide us to discipline them in loving ways.

What do you do that makes your children angry? Why do you do it? How can you discipline your children without making them angry?

13

■ WAIT FOR ME

Ps. 40:1-11: "I waited patiently for the Lord's help; then he listened to me and heard my cry" (v. 1).

We know how hard it is for children to wait—for a birthday, Christmas, a vacation. In our age of "instant everything," it's hard for us to wait too. We want something to happen right away. If we have to wait too long in line, we try a different store, a different bank teller, a different gas station.

Sometimes we carry this same impatience over into our relationship with God. We may bring a family problem to him in prayer, asking for his help. If he doesn't deliver immediately, we may get angry or question the value of prayer or the availability of God's help.

At times like this we need to remember that God is not our errand boy. He is God. As Sherwood Wirt says, "He is not wired to human controls. He is omnipotent, immortal, immutable, all-wise, all-knowing, the sovereign majesty, the Creator of the heavens and the earth. He moves at his own good pleasure, and he demands that we wait."

God's ways are not our ways. His long-range goal is to transform us into his image, and that may mean that we have to learn to wait. If we do that, our experience will be that of the psalmist: "Then he listened to me and heard my cry."

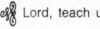 Lord, teach us to wait for you.

What does it mean for you right now to wait for God?

■ HELP OF THE HELPLESS

Psalm 46: "God is our shelter and strength, always ready to help in times of trouble" (v. 1).

A hospital chaplain visited the room of an elderly woman dying of cancer. "Pastor," she said, "I feel so helpless."

"Let me confess something to you," the pastor said. "I feel helpless too. I wish I could take your pain away and make you well again. I can't. But could we two helpless ones pray together?"

We may feel just as helpless when facing some of the problems of our children, not only health problems, but those involving relationships with other children or with a teacher. We wish we could wave a magic wand and make the problems disappear. We wish we could spare our children the pain of working through problems. But we can't.

Fortunately for us, God's grace makes it possible for us to admit our limitations. We don't have to be "superparent." We can confess to ourselves, to God, and to our children that we can't help.

Perhaps at that time we can follow the example of the hospital chaplain and pray for and with our children, committing the problem to God, "the Help of the helpless." And we can continue to pray.

Our children may have to face problems without us, but because of our intercession with God, they need not face problems alone.

 Lord, we admit that we often feel helpless before our children's problems. At such times, deepen our trust in your power and presence.

Are there situations in which you feel frustrated at being unable to help your children? How can you seek God's help together?

■ GOD'S HEALING POWER

Luke 8:40-56: "Don't be afraid; only believe, and she will be well" (v. 50).

One of the great stresses we experience as a family is sickness—the sleepless nights, the child's pain, the parents' fears. Any parent who has experienced this will be able to empathize with the father who threw himself at Jesus' feet, asking help for his only daughter, now dying at home. We feel his world collapse when the blunt message comes: "Your daughter has died."

Jesus speaks a healing word to the father's numbed heart: "Don't be afraid; only believe, and she will be well." Jesus demonstrates God's power to love even beyond the boundaries of death.

When our children are sick, we need to hear that word too. Naturally we will do all we can to see that they receive the best medical care. But we have additional power to draw on, the healing power of God released through prayer. God promised through James: "This prayer made in faith will heal the sick person; the Lord will restore him to health" (James 5:15). God's healing power is exercised through doctors and nurses, through psychologists and psychiatrists, through prayer and what we call miracles, and through his ultimate cure—the resurrection.

Lord, when sickness strikes our family, help us trust in your healing power.

Pray now for any specific health needs in your family—and thank God for the health you have.

■ ALL YOUR NEEDS

Phil. 4:19-20: "And with all his abundant wealth through Christ Jesus, my God will supply all your needs" (v. 19).

For a long time we have acted as if there would always be enough of everything—land, trees, animals, coal, oil, food. Now the time when there seemed to be unlimited resources is at an end. We see the rising cost of living, energy shortages, the staggering cost of medical care, and wonder, "Are we going to make it?" In the face of this economic anxiety, we have Paul's confident assurance: "My God will supply all your needs."

Maybe it's important in our still-wealthy society to note that God promises to supply all our *needs,* not necessarily all our *greeds.* Bombarded by advertising and peer pressure, we easily lose sight of what are really our needs.

For most of us, this economic anxiety can be kept under control, not only by trusting God, but also by actively cultivating a "holy contentment." We need to heed the encouragement: "having food and clothing, let us be content."

When God promises to supply all our needs, he has in mind more than our physical needs. Through our relationship with Jesus Christ and his body, the people of God, he gives us meaning for life and the assurance of his everlasting love.

O Lord, assure us that you will indeed supply all our needs.

Have a family discussion on how to conserve God's blessings in your home.

■ TWO LITTLE WORDS

James 5:13-18: "So then, confess your sins to one another and pray for one another . . ." (v. 16).

A friend of ours was reprimanding his 12-year-old son for neglecting some family tasks. The boy continued making excuses until the father said, "All I want you to do is to say 'I'm sorry.'"

The boy replied, "Why should I? I never hear you say that."

The father decided the 12-year-old had a point—and he determined to change.

Perhaps nothing can contribute so much to family harmony than those two little words, "I'm sorry." We often need to say them to one another as husband and wife, and there are times when we need to say them to our children too.

Sometimes we're uptight because of fatigue or sickness or some situation that has nothing to do with the children. When a child does some little thing wrong, we overreact and lash out at the child.

As soon as we gain control of our emotions again, we should take the child aside, explain why we flew off the handle, and ask the child's forgiveness. We needn't fear that our children will lose respect for us. We will only gain their respect—and their love. We will also make it easier for them to say "I'm sorry" to one another—and to us.

 O God of mercy, give us the courage to say "I'm sorry," especially to our children.

Have you ever apologized to your children? What was the result?

18

■ BUILD ONE ANOTHER UP

Eph. 4:29-32: "Use . . . only helpful words, the kind that build up" (v. 29).

Sticks and stones may break my bones, but words can never harm me," we used to chant as children. But even then we knew it was a lie. Words can and do hurt us; they can destroy our self-confidence and make us shrivel up inside. But words can also heal, encourage, and build us up.

Our words give us great power over our children—power to hurt or to help. Christian psychologist Bruce Narramore says, "Every criticism is a blow to a child's self-image. Each compliment helps to build an inner sense of confidence."

There are times when we must criticize our children as part of the discipline we have to provide. But we can try to do that gently, without using words that insult or tear down or humiliate. And we can try to keep our faultfinding to a minimum, concentrating on the problems that count.

Most important of all, we can build our children's self-image by expressing appreciation and love, by complimenting them when they do well, by letting them know they are valued members of the family.

If you're like us, you find it easier to criticize than to compliment. We need to remind ourselves often to use words that recognize and encourage all the wonderful, helpful, funny things our children do.

Lord of love, let our words be helpful, the kind that build up our children.

Write down what you like about each of your children. This will help you find the words to build up a child's positive self-image.

■ CITIZENS OF HEAVEN

Phil. 3:17-21: "We, however, are citizens of heaven" (v. 20).

For four years we served as missionaries on the island of Madagascar. While we were happy to be there, we always knew that we didn't really belong. No matter how we tried, we were always different. We remained citizens of the United States, aliens in another country.

Paul says that Christians are citizens of heaven. Our ultimate loyalty is not to any earthly government, but to the kingdom of God. Therefore, we live by values and customs different from those of our society, values we try to teach to our children.

This means that we and our children may not always "fit in," that we will always be to some extent "outsiders." This may be hard because it is natural for children to want to be like everyone else, to feel a part of a group. We don't want them to be hurt or shut out.

Yet it is important for us to teach our children that Christians have different values. We can try to strengthen them by our teaching and example. We can give them opportunities to feel a sense of belonging with Christian friends.

We and our children may be outsiders and aliens, but we have something far more important and lasting —our citizenship in heaven. And someday we will go home.

 Lord God, thank you for our citizenship in heaven. Help us to live as citizens of heaven, loyal to you and to your kingdom.

In what ways do you believe God wants you to be different from the society in which you live?

■ HELPED TO HELP

2 Cor. 1:3-4: "He helps us in all our troubles, so that we are able to help others who have all kinds of troubles" (v. 4).

What do we do when we see another family having trouble? Do we cluck our tongues and feel superior? Or do we try to find a way to help?

Nothing teaches like experience. When we've worked through a family crisis—a discipline problem, the death of a family member, dealing with a handicapped child—then, especially, we are in a position to help others.

Helping is not always easy, though, and there are pitfalls. We will want to be sensitive to the other family. If we have the kind of personality that wants to "fix" other people, we may have to curb our impulses. On the other hand, if we are shy or worried about how we will be received, we may need to take extra courage.

It is usually not helpful to pretend we know all the answers. We can begin by just sharing our struggles, our failures, our disappointments. Sometimes the best thing to do is simply to listen. Sometimes lending a book which has helped us may be a nonthreatening way to offer suggestions.

All this works two ways. When we're having a family problem, we don't have to go it alone. We can admit that we need help and seek it from another family. Through them God may offer us his help.

 Lord, enable us both to give and to receive help.

In what areas of family life do you feel you could offer help? In which areas might you receive help from another family?

■ DON'T KID YOURSELF

James 1:22-25: "Do not deceive yourselves by just listening to his word; instead, put it into practice" (v. 22).

A friend who was having serious problems relating to her children once came to us for advice. We suggested the book *Between Parent and Child* by Haim Ginott. After reading the book, the friend said, "Well, what he says is just common sense!"

We replied, "Yes, but are you *doing* what he says?" She had to admit that she wasn't.

The Bible also gives us good advice—for family living and for all situations of life. But just hearing that Word, or reading it, is not enough; we must put it into practice, as James says.

Jesus said, "If you obey my teaching, . . . you will know the truth, and the truth will set you free." James suggests several steps to help us do this: look *closely* into the perfect law that sets people free; keep on paying attention to it; don't forget it, but put it into practice. Then, he says, you will be blessed by God in what you do. As we act on the wisdom we have, God will set us free from our mistakes as parents, our own shortcomings and selfishness, our bad habits and inconsistencies. He will set us free to be better husbands and wives and parents.

Help us, Lord, to be not only hearers of your Word, but also doers.

Make a list of the things you feel you are doing well as parents. When you're tempted to dwell too much on your failures, remember this list!

■ THE FAITH WE HAVE

Mark 9:14-29:   "I do have faith, but not enough.
Help me have more!" (v. 24).

We find it easy to identify with these parents. In
desperation they bring their sick child to Jesus. Even
the disciples had been unable to heal him. Now
Jesus is their only hope.

Jesus makes a ringing statement on the power of
faith: "Everything is possible for the person who has
faith." The father seems to accept this idea, but his
problem is that he doesn't have much faith left. His
little boy has been sick for so long; all attempts at
healing have failed. So he cries out, "I do have faith,
but not enough. Help me have more."

We too need faith, not only in a time of crisis, but
in the daily demands of parenthood. We too may know
that faith has great power. But often we don't have
faith to move mole hills—much less mountains.
What can we do then? We can come to God with the
faith we have, even if it is so little we wonder if it's
real. For the real power is not in our faith, but in
God, who is greater than our weakness. We can act
on the faith we have, and we can, like this father,
cry out, "Help me have more."

O God, increase our faith. Enable us to put
into practice the faith we have and teach us to
trust you more.

Is there a situation in your family life in which you
are having a hard time trusting God? Plan together
what to do about it.

■ LITTLE CHILD LOST

Matt. 18:10-14: "Your Father in heaven does not want any of these little ones to be lost" (v. 14).

We had just checked into Dulles International Airport on our way to Madagascar with our three little children. On our way to the waiting area we were concentrating on our month-old baby and our hand luggage. Suddenly we realized our four-year-old daughter was missing. With a tight feeling in my stomach I retraced our steps, scanning the crowds for her little blond head.

Then the loudspeaker crackled: "Mr. Ronald Klug, we have a little girl looking for her father." I ran to the counter where the police were trying to comfort a sobbing, red-faced Rebecca. I knew I didn't have to reprimand her or warn her; I was happy just to hug her and dry her tears.

Any parent who has ever searched for a lost child and known the joyful relief of finding one can understand God's concern for his lost children. He does not just wait for his wandering children to return. He seeks us out, calling to us through the incidents of our lives, through the feelings of our hearts, through other people, through his Word. And when we return to him, our relationship restored, he rejoices and welcomes us back with open arms.

Heavenly Father, we are grateful that you keep searching for us over and over.

In what ways have you felt God searching for you?

■ THE VALUE OF PRAISE

1 Chron. 16:8-10: "Sing praise to the Lord; tell the wonderful things he has done" (v. 9).

One of the most beautiful things in the world is praise, especially when we compare it to its opposites—complaining, faultfinding, grumbling. If we want truly happy homes, let them be houses of praise.

We know that our children need our praise, yet we're so quick to point out their faults and so slow to commend them. But it is praise that will give them the positive self-image that will help them grow into confident, productive, loving adults.

We parents need praise from one another. In the stresses and difficulties of the day, spirits can be lifted by a word of praise for a good dinner, a clean house, a well-kept yard, a helpful way of solving a problem.

Then let our praise move out into our community and the world. Although we all face many difficult problems, we can encourage the good, rejoicing in the progress and achievements of those who are working to create a better world, expressing our appreciation and support.

Then, above all, praise the one who gives all these good gifts. In prayers and songs and lives of service, praise the Lord!

✺ Lord, fill our lives with praise.

Just for today, be lavish with praise—to God, to one another, and to each of your children.

■ BUILDING FOR THE FUTURE

Jer. 29:4-14: "I alone know the plans I have
for you" (v. 11).

Some 700 years before the birth of Jesus, the powerful
state of Babylon invaded the Jewish homeland, taking
many Jewish people as slaves. Suddenly the Jews
found themselves as refugees, strangers in a strange
land. How were they to live their lives in an alien
culture?

Through his prophet Jeremiah God told them,
"Build houses. Settle down. Plant gardens. Marry and
have children. Work for the good of the cities. Pray to
me on their behalf." In other words, they were to
carry out all the regular activities of life, and they
were to help improve the communities in which they
were living.

In a sense we Christians are also strangers in a
strange land, especially as we see our society moving
more and more away from Christian values. To many,
disaster seems to loom on the horizon. Yet we are not
to give up, withdraw, and sit pessimistically waiting
for the end. Rather God calls us to go on working
for the welfare of our families and our communities,
trusting that he has a plan for us that includes
"prosperity and not disaster."

Martin Luther was asked, "What would you do if
you knew Jesus would return tomorrow?"

He replied, "I would go out and plant a tree."

Eternal Lord, help us build for the future, trusting
in your care.

**Identify the ways you are working for the good of the
community in which God has placed you.**

■ LOOK OUT FOR OTHERS

Phil. 2:1-11: "Look out for one another's interests, not just for your own" (v. 4).

The racks are full of books that tell us *How to Take Care of No. 1* and *How to Be Sure to Get What You Want*. Pop psychologists encourage us to meet our own needs at the expense of others. This is a good formula for turning a family into a battleground; it's a formula that is destroying many families.

The Bible proclaims the opposite wisdom. The Christian's stance is not, "I have *my* rights, and I'm going to see that *my* needs are met." Rather it is, "You have *your* rights, and I'll help you see that *your* needs are met."

To be sure, there is a legitimate self-concern. Parents do need to get enough sleep, for example, or find time for spiritual growth. But our major focus is always on meeting the needs of our children and one another. In this way our children too will learn to care for one another—and for us. Our motive and model for this self-giving is Jesus, who emptied himself of his rights and became a servant to all.

Mother Teresa of Calcutta has said, "If you learn the art of being thoughtful, you will become more and more Christ-like, for his heart was meek and always thought of others."

Lord, motivate us with the power of Jesus and guide us to serve one another.

List the special needs of each family member and how each of you can help.

■ TIME FOR YOUR MARRIAGE

Eph. 5:21-33: "The two will become one" (v. 31).

The demands on our time seem endless. The children need us. The schools need us. The neighborhood needs us. The church needs us. Our political party needs us. But in all our struggles to find enough time, let us not forget that as a couple we need one another.

In most cases the best thing we can do for our children is to have a good marriage. Children need the security of living with parents who are secure in one another's love.

A marriage takes time, and we need not feel guilty because we need and want time together for a quiet meal or an evening or weekend away from the children. Even at an early age children can understand that parents need time "alone together." (They need time away from us too.) No amount of "doing things for the children" can make up for the security of a loving home.

We believe God has brought us together and made us one. In the time we take to nourish our marriage, his Spirit is at work to draw us closer together and increase our unity.

O Lord our God, we thank you for making us one. Thank you for our time alone.

Schedule some "alone together" time for this week.

■ FORGIVING OURSELVES

1 John 3:19-24: "If our conscience condemns us, we know that God is greater than our conscience and that he knows everything" (v. 20).

The more conscientious we are as parents, the more we feel like failures. We're conscious of our irritability, our impatience, our lack of wisdom, our selfishness. We may read books of advice and end up feeling so inadequate we wonder whether we were really cut out to be parents—only now it's too late to do anything about it!

Some people today respond by wanting to get rid of the idea of sin. They don't want to recognize that sometimes we are wrong and do wrong. The Bible is more realistic; it says, "If we say that we have no sin, we deceive ourselves" (1 John 1:8).

But there is no need for despair or deception. We can admit our failures and our willfulness and reassure ourselves of God's forgiveness. Then we can go on to accept that forgiveness.

Novelist Elizabeth Goudge wrote in *A Cry in the Snow:* "There is no one harder to forgive than oneself; it can take years. Nevertheless we know inside ourselves that it must be done, for remorse is a sin that rots at the vitals of the soul. And we know well the price of a soul to God. If God and his saints in their divine foolishness put such a price upon our soul, we should not let it rot."

When our conscience drives us to despair, remind us that your love and forgiveness are greater. Enable us to forgive ourselves for Christ's sake.

Reassure one another of God's forgiveness.

■ THE EYE OF THE STORM

Mark 4:35-41: "The wind died down, and there was a great calm" (v. 39).

One day when our daughter was four years old we read together a children's Bible story about Jesus stilling the storm. A half hour later we were walking to the store. It was a windy day. Rebecca amazed me by saying, "In *this* world when you tell the wind to stop blowing, it doesn't stop. This is a bad world."

Already as a small child she could see that we cannot always expect good to triumph so easily. There is a great mystery about evil that leaves us all with unanswered and agonizing questions.

Yet while we cannot control the weather with a word, we can trust in God's power in the midst of life's storms. Leslie Weatherhead wrote: "If God allows calamity to happen—as he does—he can cope with it. He can make evil serve the end of man's blessedness as powerfully as good."

We find, as Christians have through the ages, that Jesus can restore calm to our minds and hearts. Even in the worst of the storm we hear his strong voice say to us, "I am with you in this 'bad world.' Peace. Be still."

 Lord, in all the storms of life, help us look to you. Calm our troubled minds, and let your peace rule in our hearts.

What is the biggest "storm" your family has weathered in the past? How did God's help come to you then?

■ NO PLACE LIKE HOME

John 8:34-36: "A slave does not belong to a family permanently, but a son belongs there forever" (v. 35).

In his poem "The Death of a Hired Man," Robert Frost tells of an old man who returns to the farm where he had worked years before, the farm which is his only home. Frost says, "Home is the place where, when you have to go there, they have to take you in."

Jesus has promised, "I will never turn away anyone who comes to me" (John 6:37). This gives us the security of knowing that no matter what we have done we can always return to him.

Our children need this assurance about home, the security of knowing there is one safe place, one place where they do not have to earn favor, one place where they will always be loved and accepted and welcomed. Home should be the one place where "love never gives up" (1 Cor. 13:7).

Charlie Shedd has written: "We must get it across— 'You can never do anything so dreadful, say anything so terrible, be anything so awful, but that we still love you.'"

 Heavenly Father, we're grateful that your love never lets us go. Help us communicate that kind of unconditional love to our children.

Right now plan a specific way to let your children know that your love for them is forever.

■ THE FAMILY OF GOD

Matt. 12:46-50:   "Whoever does what my Father in heaven wants him to do is my brother, my sister, and my mother" (v. 50).

We hear much talk today about the "extended family" and how grandparents and uncles and aunts and cousins are needed to shore up the nuclear family of parents and children. We may feel the need for such support, yet not be able to receive it because we live too far from our relatives.

As Christians we have an extended family in the church. God has called us into this great family, and here we may find brothers and sisters and fathers and mothers who are closer to us than our biological families because they share our faith and values and because we can be together more often. Particularly in times of crisis, we may find this church family surrounding us, encouraging, supporting, and offering practical help.

Through the church our family is extended to include single people, the elderly, other families, children in need of friendship, or lonely and neglected adults. As we open our hearts and lives to these people, each member of our extended church family can become a unique gift of God for us and our children.

Heavenly Father, we thank you for our extended family in the Christian church. Help us to open our family and include those who need us and who can enrich our lives.

Make a list of the members of your "extended family." What specific things can you do for each of them?

■ BE STILL

Ps. 37:3-9: "Be still before the Lord and wait patiently for him" (v. 7 NIV).

A boy and his father went hunting in the woods. After they had hunted together a while, they decided to split up. The father said, "You stay here. I'll come back and find you. Just wait for me."

After what seemed like a long time, the boy became convinced that his father had left without him. He started crashing through the brush, trying to find his way home. He wandered around in circles, growing more and more panicky. Finally exhausted, he sat down, on the verge of tears. As he sat there quietly, he heard his father calling to him. He shouted back, and soon father and son were reunited.

Faced with a problem in our family, we can so easily exhaust ourselves running around in circles, growing more desperate and frustrated. We may need to stop thrashing about, take time to be quiet in God's presence. Then we can hear our Father's voice saying, "Be still, and know that I am God" (Ps. 46:10 NIV).

Then for a time we take our eyes off the problem and think about God, reminding ourselves what we know about him, who he is, what he has done for us. We can assure ourselves of his power and presence with us now. We wait, believing that if we listen, we will hear.

O God, teach us to be still long enough to hear your voice.

Can you recall some problems that were solved after you stopped "thrashing about"?

■ ONE IN SOUL AND MIND

Phil. 2:1-2: ". . . being one in soul and mind" (v. 2).

A two-year-old toddles to mother with a request for candy. When she says no, he tries daddy. Children know which parent to ask and how to play one off against the other.

In many small matters this may be relatively harmless. But for the more important issues, it is imperative that parents be of one mind. Time spent working for that kind of unity will be well worth it in the many problems that will be avoided.

Such unity is not always easy to achieve. Parents may come from different backgrounds and have different personalities. They will not always think and feel exactly alike. Although these differences may be a strength which enables one parent to succeed where another cannot, it is important to talk *together* about your family life, your goals, your discipline patterns, your schedule. This is made much easier when both parents share a common foundation of faith in God.

Perhaps your discussion will not always lead to total agreement, but just learning to understand one another will help family harmony. One writer put it this way: "The goal in marriage is not to think alike, but to think together."

O Spirit of peace, grant us unity of mind where we most need it.

Can you identify one area in family life where you disagree? Try to understand why your spouse sees it a different way.

■ THE PRESENT MOMENT

2 Cor. 6:1-2: "Listen! This is the hour to receive God's favor; today is the day to be saved!" (v. 2).

A middle-aged man once told me with sadness, "Until recently I lived in the future. I looked forward to the time when I would graduate from school, when I would get married, when I would get that special job. Now I find I'm already living in the past. I've never learned to live in the present."

It's possible for us to make the same mistake in living with our children. When they are small, we may look forward to the time when they will be less dependent on us, perhaps when they go to school. Then, as each year passes, they more often want to be with their friends, and we begin to wish they would spend some time with us. Children really do grow up very fast!

We can learn to see in each period of a child's life a special moment, with unique joys and responsibilities. We can learn to accept our children— and ourselves—as we are at the present moment.

Now is the time to enjoy life with our children. Now is the time to let our children know that we love them. Now is the time to share our faith in God with them. Now is the time to thank God for our children and for one another.

 Lord, teach us how to make the most of the present moment.

List three ways in which you can make the most of your present family situation.

■ THE OLD, OLD STORY

2 Tim. 3:14-17: "Ever since you were a child you have known the Holy Scriptures" (v. 15).

In his trenchant style Martin Luther once exclaimed: "The mother who tells the story of her Lord is a better preacher than the Archbishop of Mainz."

One of our privileges and obligations as Christian parents is to pass on to our children the heritage of the Bible. Even at an early age children like Bible stories—especially if they are read or told in a context of love, simply as good stories without too much concern with teaching. Parents should especially avoid using a Bible story as an excuse for criticizing a child. Let the emphasis in the story be on what God has done in the lives of his people—and on what he does for us.

As our children grow older and can read for themselves, we will still want to continue sharing God's Word with them, perhaps in a time of family devotions. We can also give them some of the Bible story books now available—and also books of prayers and other Christian writings.

When we do this, we are doing far more than entertaining our children or merely passing on religious knowledge. For the Spirit of God does his transforming work through his Word, "so that the person who serves God may be fully qualified and equipped to do every kind of good deed."

O God, we thank you for the gift of your Word. Help us to share it with our children.

In what ways are you sharing God's Word with your children? Are there new ways you could use?

■ LISTENING TO ANOTHER

Ps. 27:7-14: "Hear me, Lord, when I call to you!" (v. 7).

A troubled teenager came home from school each day wanting to talk to her mother. "Don't bother me, I'm busy," the mother retorted. When the girl tried talking with her older brothers and sisters, she was told, "Get lost!" She did—she ended up as a teenage alcoholic.

It's a fortunate child whose mother is willing to sit and listen to the triumphs and tragedies of the day. That child is blessed who has a father willing to take a long walk and listen to the pains of life that even a young child can be experiencing.

Sometimes parents are more willing to listen than children are to talk—especially in the early years of adolescence—and we may have to accept that. One thing we can do is to build the habit of listening when the children are younger, especially by listening at the times when *they* want to talk. But it's never too late to start.

We all need someone to listen to us at times. We need God to listen to us—and he has promised to do just that.

Listening to our children may take special time and effort. But our reward may be that if we listen to our children, they will come to us when they need help and sometimes they will listen to us!

 Make us good listeners, Lord.

Plan how you could spend more time listening to your children.

■ WHAT DO I DO NOW?

James 1:5-8: "If any of you lacks wisdom, he should pray to God" (v. 5).

A child complains of a stomachache in the morning. Or gets beat up at school. Or stays out late without permission. A child says, "I hate you" or "I don't believe in God." "What do we do now?" we ask ourselves over and over.

If only we were wiser, we think. So we ask friends and read books and attend classes—and sometimes end up being more confused than when we started.

But there is something we can do: we can convert our confusion into prayer. James wrote, "If any of you lacks wisdom, he should pray to God." In the midst of our need, we can turn to God, ask for wisdom, and trust that he will provide it, perhaps through the word of a friend, a counselor, or a book or article.

Sometimes, it's true, we may receive contradictory advice, or advice that doesn't seem to fit for us. Here's where we have to trust God and follow the advice that "feels" right to us as unique parents with unique children.

James's encouragement to pray includes a trustworthy promise: "If any of you lacks wisdom, he should pray to God, who will give it to him; because God gives generously and graciously to all."

O God, we need wisdom to make right decisions in our family, and we trust that you will provide it.

Identify a confusing or troublesome problem in your family life. Pray now that God will give you the wisdom to handle it in the best way.

■ THE POWER THAT CHRIST GIVES

Phil. 4:12-13: "I have the strength to face all conditions by the power that Christ gives me" (v. 13).

A friend was paralyzed in a surfing accident. Given only a slight chance of ever moving again, he experienced a miraculous recovery. During the months of painful rehabilitation, Phil. 4:13 was his favorite Bible verse.

As parents we need this strength too—especially in a crisis, when a child is injured or critically ill, when we face a serious discipline problem or a breakdown in family relationships. At such times we naturally cry out to God, and perhaps because we are so helpless, he responds graciously with the courage and wisdom we need.

But we need the strength of God also when facing the "daily-ness" of life with children—the constant struggle with messy rooms or lost shoes or less-than-polite table manners or problems with homework. Then it's the constancy of the problem that wears us down.

How important, then, that we take time for prayer, placing ourselves in God's presence and turning to him trustfully. If we do that habitually, we will find that God is faithful and we will be able to say with Paul: "I have the strength to face all conditions by the power that Christ gives me."

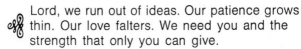 Lord, we run out of ideas. Our patience grows thin. Our love falters. We need you and the strength that only you can give.

On a card write the words, "I have the strength to face all conditions by the power that Christ gives me." Tape the card where you can see it during the day.

■ BEWARE OF STRANGERS?

Heb. 13:1-3: "Remember to welcome strangers in your homes" (v. 2).

In many areas of family life we walk a tightrope, balancing between two dangers. Sometimes for the sake of our children's safety we must warn them, teaching them to fear strangers who would offer them a ride or lure them with candy. At the same time we don't want them to fear all new people or all who are different. We want our children to move among people with openness and confidence—and at the same time with respect and caution.

This is a special challenge for God's people. Already in the Old Testament God's chosen people Israel were told to care for strangers and the poor, since they had been strangers in Egypt. In the New Testament Paul wrote, "You . . . are not . . . strangers any longer; you are now . . . members of the family of God" (Eph. 2:19).

Thus we bear a special responsibility for the stranger, who may be a new family in our church or in our community. We can reach out to them with a welcoming word, an invitation to our home, a ride to a store. Many Christians have sponsored refugee families or welcomed foreign students into their homes at holiday time.

Opportunities abound. As our children see us welcoming the stranger, they too will learn to be open to the great variety of God's people.

Heavenly Father, help us to open our hearts and our homes to the strangers among us.

During the coming week invite a "stranger" into your home.

■ ROOTS

Eph. 3:14-20: "Have your roots and foundation in love" (v. 17).

There's much talk of roots today. Because of our mobility and the rapid rate of change in our society, people feel the need for something of permanence.

Roots are important. Rootlessness is a painful experience, and people that are uprooted, like plants, may wilt and die. We feel especially impermanent when we or those close to us move from house to house, city to city, state to state, or even country to country. Our children may find friendships dissolved, and they may be able to visit grandparents and uncles and aunts only occasionally.

There are some simple things we can do to give our children a sense of "rootedness." We can visit places where parents or grandparents have lived. We can develop family photo albums. We can trace and record our family tree. We can write letters. We can visit churches where we were baptized or confirmed or married. We can share stories and music and food of our ethnic heritage.

Most of all, says the apostle, "Have your roots and foundations in love." Even when our children are facing many kinds of change, we can give them roots in the love of God and in our love for them.

In the midst of all that changes, O Lord, teach us to find our truest roots in your love.

Decide on an action that will help provide roots for your children.

41

■ HE BELONGS TO THE LORD

1 Sam. 1:19-28: "I asked him for this child, and he gave me what I asked for. So I am dedicating him to the Lord. As long as he lives, he will belong to the Lord" (vv. 27-28).

Hannah had prayed earnestly for a child. God heard her prayer and gave her the gift of a son. In gratitude Hannah dedicated her son to God. When he was old enough, young Samuel went to the temple, and later he became a prophet, Israel's last judge, and the anointer of Israel's first king.

We too can dedicate our children to God. We may do it in church through a rite of dedication or through baptism. Then as our children grow, we can continue to declare, "As long as he lives, he will belong to the Lord."

This means that we let go of a possessive love for our children, one which is used to meet our own needs. We let go of our own plans which we might be tempted to impose in our children.

By saying, "Our children belong to the Lord," we set them free to develop according to God's unique plan for each child.

Then we can relax a bit. We do not have to carry more responsibility than is rightly ours. The ultimate responsibility is not ours. Our children belong to the Lord—and he will guide their destinies.

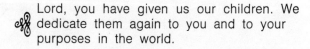 Lord, you have given us our children. We dedicate them again to you and to your purposes in the world.

Remember the days on which your children were first baptized or dedicated to God. On this day give each child a special symbol of God, like a cross.

42

■ ABBA, FATHER

Gal. 4:4-7: "To show that you are his sons, God
sent the Spirit of his Son into our hearts, the Spirit
who cries out, "Father, my Father" (v. 6).

The high point in my day," a friend remarked, "is
when I come home from work and hear my son call
'Daddy!' "

The Bible teaches us to pray to God as *Abba,* an
Aramaic word meaning "Daddy," the familiar loving
word of a child. Jesus himself used that word when
he prayed in the Garden of Gethsemane. "*Abba,*
Father," he said, "everything is possible for you"
(Mark 14:36 NIV). And Paul says that Christians
have the Spirit of Jesus dwelling within, and when we
pray, the Spirit cries, "*Abba,* Father" (Gal. 4:6 NIV).

We do not come fearfully to prayer. Jesus taught us
to pray, "Our Father . . . , " and Martin Luther
explains, "Here God encourages us to believe that he
is truly our Father and we are his children. We
therefore are to pray to him with complete confidence
just as children speak to their loving father."

We hope our children feel free to come to us and ask
us about their needs. Our heavenly Father is even
more willing to hear us and to respond with a
father's love.

 Our heavenly Father, we thank you that we
can come simply and confidently to you as
children to a loving parent.

**When family problems arise, bring them quickly
to your loving Father.**

43

■ ON TEACHING DECISION MAKING

Phil. 1:9-11: " . . . so that you will be able to choose what is best" (v. 10).

One of the most important skills we can foster in our children is the ability to make wise decisions. When they are very small, we may have to make many decisions for them. But the time comes soon enough when they make some decisions beyond our control. We want them to choose wisely regarding friends, moral issues, school subjects, careers, marriage partners. We cannot choose for them, but we can prepare them for decision making.

The only way to do this is to give them opportunities to make their own choices. Already when they are young they are capable of making small choices—in foods, clothes, toys, books. As they mature, they can make more and more of their own decisions. This means we must be free enough to allow them to make mistakes and loving enough to accept their decisions, even if they are different from what we would have done. That is the way God treats us.

In his prayer for the Philippians Paul asks that they grow in love, in knowledge, and in judgment. The result, he says, is that "your lives will be filled with the truly good qualities which only Jesus Christ can produce, for the glory and praise of God."

 Heavenly Father, give us the freedom and the courage to allow our children to make choices. Give them the wisdom to choose wisely.

Together think of ways in which you could allow your children to make more of their own decisions.

■ WHO'S YOUR AUDIENCE?

Col. 3:23-25: ". . . as though you were working for the Lord and not for men" (v. 23).

Who is the audience to which you are playing? When you make a decision, do you find yourself wondering, "What will so-and-so think of this?" As you perform a task, do you compare yourself with others? Do you wonder, "What does *she* think about my housekeeping?" or, "What do *they* think of the way I'm raising my children?"

Those are useful questions that can make us more aware of how we function. But it's also possible for us to get so caught up in worrying about what neighbors or friends will think that we may not do what is best for our family. Or we may be so anxious about pleasing others that we become uncomfortable with our own children and unsure how to act.

Paul declares, "Christ is the real Master you serve." And he encourages us to work "for the Lord and not for men." When we do that, we're free to serve the one who has given us the task of child-rearing. We can then make decisions that are right for our family, even though they may not always gain the approval of others.

 Lord, help us to remember that you are our only Master so that we are free to make wise decisions without fear of the opinion of others.

Are you tempted to do certain things in your family because of others? Can you identify the different audiences to which you are playing?

■ THE PANGS OF BIRTH

John 16:19-22: "When the baby is born, she forgets her suffering, because she is happy that a baby has been born into the world" (v. 21).

In the process of a long or difficult labor, both mother and father may vow, "Never again!" But after the birth, the mother, who suffered the most directly, is often the one who is first to think about having another. "When the baby is born, she forgets her suffering."

There are other situations too in family life where we go through some difficult birth pangs. It may be when a child is going through a troublesome stage, or struggling with serious temptations, or facing a critical illness. Then we know the pains of birth all over again. But we can be strengthened by the assurance that although birth is painful, it can lead to joy. The psalmist said, "Tears may flow in the night, but joy comes in the morning" (Ps. 30:5).

In the midst of a painful time we can continue to look to God, knowing he is always able to make a new beginning and to bring new life out of a painful situation. We can hold to his promise: "Now you are sad, but I will see you again, and your hearts will be filled with gladness, the kind of gladness no one can take away from you."

O Lord, in the midst of our pain, we look to you for new life.

Can you remember times when God brought new life to your family after a time of pain?

■ CONTINUE TO GROW

2 Peter 3:13-18: "Continue to grow in the grace and knowledge of our Lord and Savior Jesus Christ" (v. 18).

We often notice how fast our children grow. We see them shoot up physically and watch as they develop new interests, hobbies, skills.

But what about our own growth? Do we take time for that? God made us to grow and develop. Denied opportunities to grow, we feel stagnant, stifled. Given opportunities to grow, we feel more positive and energetic and we have more to give to others.

We grow as parents if we take time to think about family goals, to read good articles and books, to talk together and pray together, and to share with other families.

We also need to grow as a couple. When our marriage grows and when we grow as individuals, we can avoid boredom in our marriage.

Our personal growth may benefit our children most of all. If we are alive and stimulating, we encourage them, and we will more likely be the kind of people our children enjoy being with.

Through worship, Bible study, discussion groups, and prayer, we can grow spiritually too, that essential kind of development Paul had in mind when he encouraged us to "grow in grace and in the knowledge of our Lord and Savior Jesus Christ."

 O life-giving Spirit, keep us alive and growing.

Share the ways in which each of you is growing. Agree to help one another find time for personal growth.

■ THE JOY OF GIVING

Matt. 7:7-11: "As bad as you are, you know how to give good things to your children. How much more, then, will your Father in heaven give good things to those who ask him!" (v. 11).

It's great fun to give gifts. There's thinking about the right gift for a person, then buying or making it, and then the anticipation of the actual gift giving. Most of us enjoy giving gifts to our children at Christmas or a birthday—or the spur-of-the-moment gift that brings special delight to a child.

No matter how generous we are, our giving may still be tainted by selfishness, by the desire to manipulate, or the need to receive thanks. God is never like that. He takes delight in giving just because it is his nature to give. He gives generously, with no strings attached. From him we receive all good things: our spouse, our children, our home, health, food, and everything that makes for the full and joyful life he wants us to have.

And, as Luke says, above all else he gives the Holy Spirit, God himself in our hearts to empower and guide us (Luke 11:13).

Gracious Father, we thank you for all the gifts you have so richly given, above all for the gift of your Spirit in our lives.

Give a special gift to each child. It doesn't have to be expensive or "store-bought" to be a sign of love.

■ THE BURSTING POINT

Ps. 103:6-14: "He knows what we are made of; he remembers that we are dust" (v. 14).

We've found that if we can remember our children's limitations—and our own—we can avoid many unpleasant family problems. Often when children misbehave, it's because they've been placed in situations which they can't handle. We try, for example, to avoid dragging them in and out of stores for several hours or keeping them up beyond a reasonable bedtime or expecting them to entertain themselves beyond what's possible at their age level.

Problems can also be avoided by taking into account our own limitations as parents. We may have a low tolerance for noise. Or we may not be the kind of parents who can enjoy a half-dozen preschoolers at one time. Or we may need some time away from the children in order to enjoy the time we do spend with them. Sometimes we can let the parent with the greatest tolerance for a situation handle it.

We can accept our own limitations—and those of our children—knowing that God, who is "as kind as a father" also "remembers that we are dust."

Lord, we're thankful that you know our weaknesses and are always ready to forgive.

Identify situations in which you sometimes ignore your children's limitations, or your own. How can you better handle these?

■ BREAKING THE CYCLE

1 Peter 3:8-12: "Do not pay back evil with evil or cursing with cursing; instead, pay back with a blessing" (v. 9).

He hit me first!" And so begins a round of hitting back and name-calling.

As parents we can also be drawn into this kind of battle with a child. "He was sassy to me, so I'll show him!" And so a round of ill will begins—and continues—in a downward spiral, straining the relationship, perhaps to the breaking point.

Someone has to stop the downward spiral. Someone has to break the bad cycle. And since we are the adults with greater maturity, the responsibility falls on us—even though it may be a difficult one.

Here we have the possibility of being like God. In the face of our evil and rebellion, he broke the cycle by sending his Son to be our Savior, to break the bond of sin and free us for a new kind of life.

When we repay our children with good, we make it possible for them to do the same for one another—and for us. We make it possible for a more secure family harmony to emerge.

 We thank you, heavenly Father, that you repay our evil with blessing. Help us to do the same for our children and for one another.

Can you recall a time when someone in your family repaid evil with a blessing? What was the result?

■ ACTIONS MORE THAN WORDS

1 John 3:13-18: "Our love should not be just words and talk; it must be true love, which shows itself in action" (v. 18).

A friend once asked a group of children to identify the names they did not like to be called. First they identified "Stinky," "Fatso," and the like, but they also named "Dearie," "Sweetie," and "Honey." Children are quick to recognize when these names are used in a sentimental, condescending way that does not express real love. They know the difference between that kind of talk and "true love, which shows itself in action."

Within the family there are always many opportunities for showing love in action. One helpful guiding principle is: Instead of showing love the way *we* want to show it, we should show love the way the receiver wants to experience it. We may want to give our son a gift, but he might rather be taken to a ball game. Mother might appreciate help with the dishes more than a bouquet of flowers. A child might prefer help with a task or a special food or a trip downtown with dad.

God did more than give us words about love. He showed his love in action by entering our life in the person of Jesus. Our love can be like that too.

Lord, help us to love one another, not only with words, but also with sensitive actions.

Think of a special way in which each family member wants to be loved. At the first opportunity, show love in those special ways.

■ POSSIBLE FOR GOD

Matt. 19:16-30: "This is impossible for man, but for God everything is possible" (v. 26).

One of the worst feelings we can have is the helpless sinking conviction, "I can't do it; it's just impossible."

And there will come times in our family life when that happens. Because of the situation or our own shortcomings, we will not be able to help our children or one another as we wish.

At just such a time faith in God can give us the resiliency to keep going. We can accept the fact that we can't do it all. We can come in our helplessness to God, trusting that he can do what we cannot do. God can love our child in a way we cannot. He can forgive when we cannot. He can help when we cannot. He cares in ways that we cannot.

Sometimes he may help by changing us, giving us a new ability to cope. Sometimes he may help our children through someone else—a friend, a teacher, a relative, a stranger. Sometimes he may alter the circumstances, providing "a way out" (1 Cor. 10:13).

What we can do is to trust Jesus' promise, "for God everything is possible," and when we can no longer even believe in God and hold on to him, we can rest in the knowledge that he holds on to us. Underneath us are "the everlasting arms."

When things seem impossible to us, give us the faith to believe that for you everything is possible.

Can you remember a time when God worked out a solution to an "impossible" situation in your life?

■ BETTER FOR YOU

John 16:5-15: "It is better for you that I go away" (v. 7).

It was the evening before Jesus' death. He knew the bitter road that lay before him, and he was preparing his disciples for the time when he would no longer be physically with them. Imagine the panicky feeling of the disciples: how could they ever get along without Jesus?

Yet it was necessary for Jesus to leave them if they were to mature and achieve their destiny. By removing his physical presence from them, Jesus would make room for the coming of the Helper, the Holy Spirit. Under the influence of that Spirit, the disciples would be led into all truth and would receive power to witness and serve.

A similar situation occurs between us and our children. In order for them to reach true maturity we must let them go. After parenting them for 18 years or more, it may be hard for us to stop trying to control or change them, but it is necessary. Even while our children are young, we can remind ourselves that our job is temporary, that we are preparing them for independence.

Good parents teach their children to do without them. We do that and then release them, trusting that the Helper, the Holy Spirit, will continue to be with them.

 Heavenly Father, help us prepare our children for independence, and enable us to let go at the right time.

Think of ways in which you are preparing your children to do without you.

■ WHAT ABOUT THE FUTURE?

Rom. 8:31-39: ". . . neither the present nor the future . . . will ever be able to separate us from the love of God which is ours through Christ Jesus our Lord" (vv. 38-39).

Romans 8 is one of our favorite chapters of the Bible, with its ringing assurance that "nothing . . . will ever be able to separate us from the love of God"—not even "the future."

When we think about the future in this context, we may think first of life after death and God's continuing presence beyond the grave. But we can also apply that promise to our future here on earth.

When our children are small we may wonder, "How will we be able to handle those difficult teenage years? Will we have to face the problems of drugs, alcohol, delinquency, rebellion? Will we have a good relationship with our children after they leave home?"

Or we may worry about the future of our country and the world—inflation, war, lawlessness in the nation and abroad. It's difficult to maintain optimism in the face of so many seemingly unsolvable problems.

When our hearts are filled with fear for the future, we can reassure ourselves—not that the future will always be just as we wish it, but that no matter what happens, nothing can separate us—or our children—from God and his love.

 Lord, we thank you for this precious promise. May it strengthen us for the present and the future.

Share your vision of the future with one another. How can you find security in the promise of God's love?

■ THE MOST IMPORTANT BUSINESS

Acts 16:25-34: "Believe in the Lord Jesus, and you will be saved—you and your family" (v. 31).

Once a group of us were discussing our responsibility to society. One friend said, "One of our children is planning to be a teacher; another is a nurse; another is working with handicapped children as a physical therapist. I think we're doing a lot for society just by raising children like that."

He made a significant point. We may choose to serve society by being active in a political party or by working for change through a church group or other agency. But we also strengthen society by building our own family.

Kenneth Chafin wrote: "If the family fails, then all the other institutions of society will fail. The family is the basic unit which undergirds all else. Every influence which weakens the family and makes it more difficult for it to do the job will ultimately weaken society. All that is done to build strong, healthy, happy, and effective families will increase the possibility of a strong and healthy society. . . . The building of an effective, healthy family unit is the most important business in the world."

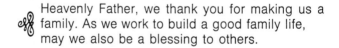

Heavenly Father, we thank you for making us a family. As we work to build a good family life, may we also be a blessing to others.

Can you see ways in which you are helping your community by building your family life?

■ SOWING AND REAPING

Gal. 6:7-10: "A person will reap exactly what he plants" (v. 7).

When his son was caught stealing pencils in school, a father chided the boy: "Why did you steal pencils? I could have brought you all the pencils you needed from the office." We reap what we sow.

When our children are misbehaving, and we want to do something about it, a good place to begin is to look at our own behavior. Such self-examination can be painful; it's easier just to blame the children. Yet our self-criticism may be the key to improving the situation.

If our children are yelling, is it because we yell at them? If they are quick to hit, is it because we hit them? If they are overly concerned with what their peers think of them, have they learned it from us? If they want all the things that other children have, do they see us being envious of others?

Fortunately there is a positive side to this: If we sow good seeds—loving ways, words of appreciation, tactful behavior, gratitude, a helpful spirit—we will reap the same from our children.

Lord, assure us of your forgiveness and enable us to examine our own lives with honesty.

Can you identify ways—positive and negative—in which you reap what you sow in your family life?

■ HONESTY AND LOVE

Matt. 5:21-24: "Go at once and make peace with your brother" (v. 24).

How do you respond when a child does something that "bugs" you? One way to respond is to blow up in anger and criticize the offender in front of the whole family, leaving the child humiliated and resentful. Another response is to play the martyr and bottle up the grievance, hoping to avoid trouble and save the relationship. But such grievances may then be converted into resentment or depression. The Bible suggests a better alternative—we can go to the person alone and discuss the problem.

It may be hard for us to do this. We may feel awkward or be afraid of the reaction we will get. It takes practice to confront other people honestly, yet without deliberately hurting them.

It's important to limit ourselves to the immediate problem and avoid statements like "you always . . ." or "you never . . ." Accusations like these shred a person's sense of self-worth and invite retaliation. It's also important to be as brief as possible.

We want to remember that our real goal is not just to "get something off our chest" or even to change the child's behavior, but to seek reconciliation, the restoration and strengthening of a relationship.

 Lord, teach us to be both honest and loving.

Is there a family situation that is especially bothering you? Decide how you can confront the other person honestly and lovingly.

■ REST FOR THE WEARY

Matt. 11:28-30: "Come to me, all of you who are tired from carrying heavy loads, and I will give you rest" (v. 28).

Someone has called the decade of life between the twenties and forties "The Tired Thirties." Often during those years the responsibilities of a growing career and the almost constant demands of small children may drain us of energy and leave us too exhausted to cope.

Psychologist James Dobson gives a good warning: "We must not permit ourselves to become weary to the bone." Are we allowing enough time for sleep? Can one parent give the other time off for "rest and relaxation"? Do we need to cut down on our involvements outside the home? Are we taking enough time for solitude and prayer? Do we need to pay more attention to our exercise and nutrition? Are there some changes we should make in our daily schedule?

There are things we can do to prevent fatigue and increase our energy and "cope-ability." We especially need to hear Jesus' invitation, "Come to me . . . and I will give you rest." His rest includes the assurance that he is with us to strengthen and uphold us. "Those who trust in the Lord for help will find their strength renewed. They will rise on wings like eagles; they will run and not get weary; they will walk and not grow weak" (Isa. 40:31).

O life-giving Spirit, give us rest and the renewal of our strength.

Are you both getting enough sleep? What can you do to help one another get enough rest and quiet time?

58

■ PRAYING FOR OTHERS

1 Tim. 2:1-7: ''I urge that petitions, prayers, requests, and thanksgivings be offered to God for all people'' (v. 1).

We awoke one morning to the sound of sirens. When we looked outside, we saw a fire engine and rescue squad pulling up to the house next door and paramedics rushing into the house. We soon learned that our 44-year-old neighbor had died suddenly, leaving his wife and two young girls, playmates of our children.

Before breakfast, with our table prayer, we prayed that God would be with this family to help them in this time of shock and sadness. At lunch when we prepared for the table prayer, our six-year-old asked us to pray again for the neighbors. At supper our five-year-old repeated the same request.

In ways like this our children learn to pray for others, committing them to God and asking for his help and guidance. In ways like this we can help our children to be more sensitive to the needs of others. And by our prayers we open the way for the release of God's power into the lives of others.

Then we should do what we can to help, but we can do it with less anxiety, knowing those for whom we pray are in God's hands. "The prayer of a good person has a powerful effect" (James 5:16).

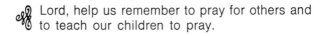 Lord, help us remember to pray for others and to teach our children to pray.

Make a list of friends, neighbors, and relatives with special needs and include them in your family prayers, maybe one each day.

59

■ THE BLESSINGS OF ORDER

1 Cor. 14:26-40: "Everything must be done in a
proper and orderly way" (v. 40).

In Paul's first letter to Corinth we get a peek into
the church life there. One of the problems was that
each person was "doing his own thing," and the result
was confusion and hard feelings. As a remedy Paul
stressed the importance of good order.

Family life can also be more pleasant and many
problems avoided when we take time to create order.
This may be the order of *place*. The old principle of
"a place for everything" makes it easier for children
to learn how to take care of their clothes and toys.
Children also seem to behave better in a neat house,
while clutter only encourages more clutter and noise.

There is also the order of *time*. Our family functions
better with a weekly and daily schedule (a flexible
one). In this way we avoid last-minute panic and
have more time for the things we really want to do.

There is also the order of *expectations*. Children
can learn to help if they know clearly what is expected
of them each day. A friend said, "This order of the
whole household eliminates the need for a lot of
nagging because the child is aware of what is expected
of him. It makes it easier for a child to be good."

Help us, Lord, to create more order in our family
to help us live more harmoniously together.

Is there a problem in your family which could be
solved by creating some order of time or place or
expectation? Plan one step for creating that order.

■ A PLACE FOR SPONTANEITY

Gal. 5:1: "Stand, then, as free people."

Our family runs best within the framework of good order. Order is helpful, yet too much can stifle love and joy. You've probably been in homes that are so neat you feel uncomfortable being there. People can become slaves to a schedule. While rules are good, the Christian life is not a slavish compulsion to rules, but a life in which we have been set free to love and serve one another.

We can live out this freedom in our family by being open to the spontaneous. There is a time to leave the dirty dishes in the sink while we take a family walk. A day can be brightened by a spur-of-the-moment decision to go to a museum or a movie. We may decide to eat out instead of cooking a meal. A long dull stretch of weeks can be broken up by a spontaneous weekend visit to friends. Some friends alleviate the boredom of a long winter by spending a weekend at a motel with a heated swimming pool. While some of these activities cost money, there are many spontaneous things to do that are free.

Such spontaneous doings may take a bit of unusual effort, and they may run the risk of an occasional failure. Yet the new and unexpected may release love and joy into our life together and create the kind of memories that make family life worthwhile.

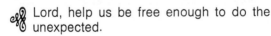 Lord, help us be free enough to do the unexpected.

Brighten this week with some spur-of-the-moment activity.

■ THE DOUBLE BIND

1 Tim. 5:3-8: "They should learn first to carry out their religious duties toward their own family" (v. 4).

When fathers and mothers get to be around 40 years old, they often find themselves in a double bind. They may be the parents of children who are approaching the difficult years of adolescence. At the same time, they may find themselves parenting their own parents who now face health problems or need to move into a nursing home or are otherwise in need of special care.

These twin responsibilities put double pressure on marriage partners. As Christians, we cannot avoid either of them. Instead, we are called to both tasks, knowing that God who gives us these responsibilities will also give the strength and wisdom to carry them out.

In facing these pressures, partners need to work together, supporting one another, encouraging one another, and making allowances for the one who is especially under pressure.

Together they can draw on God's strength and wisdom, as they seek his presence in his Word, in prayer, in Holy Communion, in the support of Christian fellowship. Together we can trust his promise: "At the time you are put to the test, he will give you the strength to endure it" (1 Cor. 10:13).

Heavenly Father, give us a special measure of strength and wisdom so that we can care for our parents at the same time that we care for our children.

Discuss the ways you are parenting your own parents. How can you help one another do this?

■ MAKE TIME FOR YOUR CHILDREN

Mark 10:13-16: "He took the children in his arms, placed his hands on each of them, and blessed them" (v. 16).

We once saw an advertising card displayed above the windows of a bus that said the average American father spends 10 minutes per week alone with his children. As a result, when children were asked to choose between their fathers and a TV set, one out of two chose the TV. The card concluded: "Make time for your children."

Someone has said, "We always have enough time for what we think is really important." If we want a good family life and a healthy relationship with our children, then we have to invest the time in it.

A worthwhile goal is for each parent to spend some time alone each day with each child, even if it is only a few minutes. Children respond warmly when they don't have to compete for our attention.

The disciples thought Jesus was too busy to spend time with children, but when Jesus realized they were sending the children away, he was angry with the disciples. He took time to give each child an individual blessing. If we take time now, we will be laying the foundation for a close and loving relationship with our children in the future.

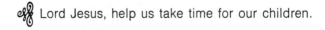 Lord Jesus, help us take time for our children.

Can you work out a schedule whereby each parent can spend time alone with each child?

63

■ THE WAITING FATHER

Luke 15:11-24: "He ran, threw his arms around his son, and kissed him" (v. 20).

This parable, surely one of the most popular in the Bible, is most often called "The Parable of the Prodigal Son." Yet perhaps a better name for it is "The Waiting Father," for Jesus used this story to show God's grace—how he gives us the freedom to choose our way in the world, and how he accepts us back when we fall.

When the son asked for his inheritance the father might well have refused, saying, "No, that's ridiculous. You're too immature to handle that much money." But he respected the son's freedom and allowed him to learn from his mistakes—a bitter lesson.

Then when the son "bottomed out" and returned, the father not only accepted him, but with a total unconcern for his own dignity ran down the road to embrace his son. And note: not a word of "I told you so" or "I hope you've learned your lesson" or "Don't let it happen again." Just new clothes and a lavish party to celebrate the return of the lost son.

What a picture of God's amazing grace. And what a model for us to follow with our own children. This picture of God gives us the courage to allow our children enough freedom, the patience to wait when they wander, and the grace to accept them back wholeheartedly, with no lectures—just love, abundant love.

 O Lord, our waiting Father, we thank you for the amazing grace you have shown us. Help us to be gracious to our children.

In what specific ways can you be more like the waiting father in the parable?

■ COPING WITH ANGER

Eph. 4:26-27: "Do not let your anger lead you into sin" (v. 26).

The children fight. A request is repeatedly ignored. A window is smashed. Result: anger!

What do we do with our anger? It's there; we needn't pretend it isn't. Psychologist Bruce Narramore says, "Anger is natural, but it isn't good."

Paul gives us two *don'ts.* "Do not let your anger lead you into sin." When we're angry, we may easily hurt a child with cutting words or harsh actions.

Paul also says, "Do not stay angry all day." Brooding only increases our anger and produces misery and resentment in a child.

What can we do with our anger then? Bottling it up may lead to depression or to frustration which later explodes. Sometimes the best immediate remedy is to remove ourselves from the situation; have our spouse take over for a while. Maybe we need to send the offending child to his room until we both calm down. We can try to find words to express our anger without damaging the child, then move on to a workable solution to the problem.

Always we can confess our anger to God and ask him to replace it with patience. Slowly but surely we can be changed.

 Lord of love, teach us how to handle our anger.

How can you help one another handle your anger in more healthy ways? A book like *Facing Anger* by Norman Rohrer and S. Philip Sutherland may help.

■ SCHOOL OF LOVE

1 John 4:11-12: "If we love one another, God lives in union with us" (v. 12).

The family is the most difficult place to live in love." Do you agree? Maybe it is good to start out with that assumption, because if we think that love within the family is easy, we will almost always become discouraged.

In other relationships we can make a temporary extra effort to be on our best behavior—and then walk away. But there is an "always-ness" in family living, and no one can keep up a good front all the time. In the family we see one another with our masks off. We know one another's faults and weaknesses, and we know how to hurt one another.

All this makes love harder in the family, yet it also makes the family the best school for love. The child who learns in the family to give and receive love, to work out conflicts, to consider the needs of others, will be well prepared to love others—and perhaps also to love God.

In the family we do not learn abstract truths about love, but we learn to love by loving and by being loved. And as we do so, we have the promise of God's presence: "If we love one another, God lives in union with us."

 Help us, heavenly Father, to make our family a school of love.

In what ways are you teaching your children to love?

■ CONFRONTING DEATH

1 Thess. 4:13-18:   "God will take back with Jesus those who have died believing in him" (v. 14).

When a neighbor whom our children affectionately called Grandma died, a host of questions was unleashed. Why did she die? Where is she now? What does her body look like? Can she still feel? Will God make her alive again? Will he give her a new body? The questions went on for days, and were often repeated.

Questions like these may make us uncomfortable. They force us to confront death in all its reality. They uncover our own doubts. They call into question our attitudes toward death and life after death.

We need to allow our children to talk about death and encourage them to share memories of the one who has died. We can avoid euphemisms like "falling asleep" or "passing away." We can listen to our children's feelings—anger at God, sorrow, guilt, fear— and help them find expression. And we can share the great hope of the resurrection, perhaps by reading a great chapter like 1 Corinthians 15 or singing an Easter hymn.

We may not be able to answer all our children's questions about death, but we can share our conviction that "we will always be with the Lord."

Thank you, Lord, for promising us victory over death.

Think ahead: how will you help your children face a death in the family or in the neighborhood?

■ YOU CAN CHANGE!

Eph. 4:17-24: "Put on the new self, which is created in God's likeness" (v. 24).

 We all tend to parent the way we were parented, to teach as we were taught—even when our parents acted in ways we didn't like. "I'm never going to do that to *my* children," we say. Then, when we get in a tight spot, we imitate the very behavior we deplored in our parents.

We may find ourselves dealing with a problem in the same way over and over again, even though it doesn't work. We keep doing it until one day we realize what's happening, analyze the situation, and come up with a better way. Then we wonder, "Why didn't I think of that before?"

We don't have to go on repeating the mistakes of our parents or our own mistakes. The good news is that with God's help we can change. Paul uses the picture of changing clothes. We can take off our old tattered clothes and put on a new suit, a new self created in God's image.

Change is not easy. It doesn't happen all at once. We may continue to slip back into old unproductive ways. We can break old habits and develop new ones, but it may be a gradual process. God is waiting for us to turn to him, to open the way for his Spirit to give us new insights and new ways of responding.

Lord, open us to new ways of being better parents.

Is there some area of parenting in which you are repeating an action that doesn't seem to work? Help one another to discover a better way.

■ WHAT ARE YOU AFRAID OF?

Isa. 41:8-13: "Do not be afraid—I am with you!" (v. 10).

Do you want your children to be afraid? Well, sometimes yes. We teach them to be afraid of sharp knives, of strangers who offer them rides, of playing in the street. But we probably don't want them to be afraid of the dark, or of all new people, or of the first day of school. Our task is to help them distinguish between realistic and unrealistic, helpful and harmful fears.

It is realistic to be afraid of a fast-moving car; it is probably not realistic to fear a lion under your bed. Helpful fears protect us from getting hurt, either physically or emotionally. Harmful fears, like the fears of public speaking or meeting new people, only mar our happiness or prevent us from becoming all we can become.

When your children are afraid, encourage them to express their fears. You should not ridicule them; their fears are as real to them as yours are to you. Let them know that it is normal to have fears; perhaps you can share some of your own and how you handle them.

Then, according to their age levels, help them sort out whether the fears are realistic or unrealistic, helpful or harmful. And give them the assurance of your help and of God's supporting presence.

Lord, show us how to handle our own fears wisely. Help us teach our children to trust in your presence.

What fears have your children expressed? How have you helped the children face them?

■ THE RIGHT TO DISCIPLINE

Eph. 6:1-3: "Children, it is your Christian duty to obey your parents" (v. 1).

God expects parents to discipline their children, and his will is that children obey. Disciplining our children is not only a duty, but a right. We may need that reminder, because many in our society tell us it is wrong to place any limits on anyone. They say everyone should be able to have everything right now, and if it feels good, do it.

It's hard not to be affected by ideas like this, so we may end up feeling guilty about our disciplining. We worry that it will "warp the child's psyche." We're concerned that if we make a mistake, we will do our children irreparable damage. We may feel we're being "undemocratic" if we "lay down the law." Or we may be afraid that we will lose our children's love or the respect of more permissive friends. We need the assurance that God himself has given us the duty and the responsibility for discipline.

To be sure, parental authority can be abused—when it is used harshly or with no consideration for the needs or developmental level of the child. Yet parental authority is still God's design for the family. Knowing that, we can discipline as wisely as we know how and trust in God's mercy to cover us when we fall short.

Lord, teach us how to discipline wisely, and thank you for your mercy when we are not wise.

When do you feel reluctant to discipline your children? Try to figure out why you feel this way.

■ THE GIFT OF PATIENCE

James 5:7-8: "See how patient a farmer is as he waits for his land to produce precious crops" (v. 7).

Have you seen the poster that says, "Lord, give me patience—and I want it right now!"? Patience has never been an easy virtue, but it seems especially hard in our time. Yet, like James' farmer, we have to plant seeds and then wait for rain, for the germination of the seeds, and then for a precious crop.

Some family problems just can't be solved, no matter how clever or strong we are. We simply have to wait them out. We need to be patient with our children, allowing them the time they need to grow. We need to be patient with one another as we struggle to become better parents. We need to be patient with ourselves, knowing God is patient with us.

We find the wisdom of *The Imitation of Christ* helpful: "Do not become angry because you cannot make others be what you think they should be, since you cannot even make yourself what you want to be."

From our own resources, we can never summon up enough patience. We must get it from God, whose patience is unlimited. He has promised patience as one of the gifts of the Holy Spirit (see Galatians 5). We pray for this gift, then wait patiently for God to give us patience!

Heavenly Father, give us a measure of your own patience.

What family situations most strain your patience? How can you help one another cope with those situations?

71

■ LIKE LITTLE CHILDREN

Matt. 18:1-5: "The greatest in the Kingdom of heaven is the one who humbles himself and becomes like this child" (v. 4).

When Jesus wanted to set up a model of the Christian, he chose a child. More than that, over the door to the kingdom of heaven he placed a sign: "Only children can enter."

We often think of the lessons we are trying to teach our children, but perhaps we have some things to learn from them. We can think of several:

The ability to forgive. We're always amazed at how soon children can forgive our anger or selfishness and how ready they are to restore the relationship.

Trust. We adults have learned to question so many things that we easily become suspicious or even cynical. Can we recover some of a child's openness to life and to other people?

Zest for life. Our two-year-old always wakes up smiling and enthusiastic about life, while we are often grouchy, thinking of the work we have to do, the problems we may have to face during the day. Maybe our children can help us to regain something of their sense of wonder and appreciation for the goodness of life.

 Heavenly Father, enable us to become like little children.

What lessons have you learned from your children?

■ RUNNING TOWARD THE GOAL

Phil. 3:12-14: "I run straight toward the goal" (v. 14).

A high school football coach once said to an uncoordinated adolescent, "If you ever got all of yourself going in the same direction at the same time, you'd be dangerous!" Sometimes it's the same with families—if only we could get them moving in the right direction! One way to do that is to set family goals, then work together to meet them.

What kind of family life do you want? What would make your family life happier? How do you think God would like to change your family? Discuss these questions together and develop a vision for your family. List the changes each person would like to see. Then from the list choose one goal; for example, if your family tends to split off in all directions, "For the next month we will spend one evening a week together." By focusing on one aspect at a time, you will be more successful than if you try to improve everything at once.

Make your goals specific. "To have a happier home" is too vague to be useful. Positive goals are better than negative ones. "To eliminate arguing at the table" is not as good as "To have each person share something good that happened each day." Pray over your goals. Look to God for the wisdom to choose and the strength to meet your goals.

 Lord, give us your vision for our family.

Try this experiment in goal setting for one month.

■ THE NAME ABOVE ALL NAMES

Matt. 1:18-25: "You will name him Jesus—because he will save his people from their sins" (v. 21).

Months before a child is born parents give much thought to choosing a name. Perhaps they consider how it sounds or what it means, or they might name the child after a special friend or relative.

God told Joseph, "Your beloved Mary will have a very special son. You will name him Jesus (which means 'God saves') because he will save his people from their sins."

God's grand plan for the human family centered on this child named Jesus, for this Jesus would show us more clearly than anything else what God is like. By his teaching, healing, feeding, rescuing, and comforting he would reveal God's love. By his death on a cross he would show how far God will go in loving us. He would be the sacrifice by which the whole world would be reconciled to God. In all these ways—and more—he saves his people from their sins. That means our sins too, including the sins we commit as parents.

St. Paul paints a great picture of the time when "in honor of the name of Jesus all beings in heaven, on earth, and in the world below will fall on their knees, and all will openly proclaim that Jesus Christ is **Lord,** to the glory of God the Father" (Phil. 2:10-11).

 Lord God, we thank you for the gift of your Son, whose name is Jesus because he is the Savior of all.

Take time to confess your sins—aloud or silently—and ask God's forgiveness.

■ A VISION OF HOPE

Matt. 28:16-20: "I will be with you always, to the end of the age" (v. 20).

What kind of a world will our children live in?" we wonder, as we think of the energy crisis, the economic problems, the threat of international war, the pollution of the earth, the erosion of decency. Some people are afraid to bring children into this kind of world, and those who have children are often afraid for them.

A wise man declared, "Where there is no vision, the people perish" (Prov. 29:18 KJV). For ourselves and for our children we need a vision of a better world— one with more emphasis on being than on having, on cooperation than on competition, a world in which we learn to care for one another and for this good earth. Then we can shape our family life to be more consistent with this vision while working with others who are striving to achieve the same goals.

If humankind were totally left to its own wisdom and devices, the prophets of doom might well be correct. But there is another factor in the picture. God, who created the universe and gives it life, promises that he will always be with us. That calms our fears. With that faith we can give our children an alternate vision, a vision of hope.

Heavenly Father, remind us that you are always with us. Give us the courage to build a better world for us and for our children.

Share your vision of what a good future would be. What are practical ways in which your family is trying to live out this vision?

■ SO KIND IS THE LORD

Ps. 103:1-14: "As kind as a father is to his children . . ." (v. 13).

A friend said, "When I was a child, I identified with the child role in our relationship to God. When I became a parent, I began to understand God's role as a father."

Being a parent *can* help us understand some basic truths about God. We can, for example, understand God's willingness to answer prayer when we realize how we want our children to come to us with their needs and problems. Jesus said, "As bad as you are, you know how to give good things to your children. How much more, then, will your Father in heaven give good things to those who ask him!" (Matt. 7:11).

We sometimes hurt with our children when we see them sick in body or mind. Sometimes, for the sake of their own growth, we have to let them make mistakes, and we suffer with them as they fumble their way through a difficult situation. In the same way, God feels our pain.

As parents we can better understand why God sometimes allows certain hard circumstances to shape our character. He does it to bless us, just as we discipline our children—for their long-term good.

In all these ways God is good to us, like a kind parent. Our own parenthood gives us clues to the nature of God, and moves us to love and trust him.

We thank you, Lord God, that you love us like a kind and good parent.

Can you think of other ways in which your experience as a parent helps you understand what God is like?

■ THANK GOD FOR PHASES!

Mark 4:26-29: "First the tender stalk appears, then the head, and finally the head full of grain" (v. 28).

An old philosopher gave us a brief phrase which can be a comfort to all parents: "This too shall pass!" It's a good phrase to remember when a child suddenly begins to act in a strange way, or drive us wild by using the latest expression over and over.

One day early in the school year our five-year-old boy started acting bossy, assertive, critical—not at all like his usually pleasant self. After several days of this we talked with a friend who said, "Well, he's acting like a typical five-year-old!"

Thank God for phases! Many "problems" are simply part of a child's normal growing stages, and they will soon disappear if we don't fuss over them too much.

There are, of course, problems that don't just go away. Books on child development can show us the normal growing stages of children and help us recognize the difference between a phase and a serious problem. Friends whose children have already gone through these stages can reassure us and give good advice.

We can accept the phases in the normal development of a child, knowing that our children are unfolding according to God's plan for growth.

Eternal Father, help us to understand the stages of a child's growth that we may trust your plan for each child.

Read a good book on child development, such as one by Arnold Gesell.

■ THE CRUCIAL HOUR

Psalm 4: "When I lie down, I go to sleep in peace" (v. 8).

Bedtime is a crucial hour in the family day. It can be a frustrating hour of battle as overtired children try every trick to stay up longer and parents' nerves become more and more frayed. Tired parents may hurry through bedtime, trying to get the children in as soon as possible so they can have a little free time for themselves.

On the other hand, bedtime can be one of the most precious times of the day. A child tucked warmly in bed when lights are low is particularly vulnerable. It's a time when a child may reveal some hurt or anxiety, as our six-year-old did when he finally poured out his fears about learning to read. It's a time when a parent may share a special word of praise, encouragement, or love for that child alone.

And when a child is relaxed, it is a good time to share a song, a story, a prayer, a tape, or a record. Psychologists tell us that thoughts planted just before sleep will continue to "work" in the subconscious throughout the night. Brother Lawrence wrote, "The ship of the soul goes forward even in sleep."

Spirit of love, help us to make bedtime a loving time for our family.

Plan together the bedtime ritual you might use for each child and how you will share the responsibilities.

■ FINDING THEIR OWN WAY

Luke 1:57-66: "What is this child going to be?" (v. 66).

Some strange events surrounded the birth of John the Baptist: an angel's announcement, a father struck dumb from unbelief, a conception in old age. It all made people wonder, "What is this child going to be?"

It's a question we can't help asking when we look at our children. We think about the future and wonder: Will he be a pilot, a teacher, a mechanic? Will she be a doctor, a homemaker, an artist? Will they be happy, loving, fulfilled?

We can't see into the future, but we can at least keep from imposing onto our children our own vision of what they ought to become. How many children have suffered by being forced or pressured into lives designed by parents!

Instead of forcing our children into molds we have chosen, we can help them discover their own talents, explore their own interests, and thus find the way in which they can make their best contribution to the human family.

God accomplished great things through the child of Zechariah and Elizabeth: he prepared the people to receive Jesus as their Savior. God can accomplish great things through our children too.

Lord, we thank you for the talents and interests you have given our children. Help us free them to do whatever you call them to do with their gifts.

Take time to recognize the talents and interests your children show at this time in their lives. Talk about how you can foster the interests.

■ DEEDS OF SIMPLE KINDNESS

John 2:1-11: "There he revealed his glory" (v. 11).

It seems a strange choice for a first miracle. One might have expected Jesus to heal a sick person, or feed a multitude, or maybe even raise the dead. Instead, Jesus saves a young couple from embarrassment by providing more wine for their wedding celebration.

We may never be called on to perform some dramatic deed that astounds the world or changes the course of history. But each day we do have the opportunity to carry out some simple act of love for our family. Perhaps it's helping with some household task, or stopping to listen to a child who has something to say that is very important to him. Maybe it's encouraging someone else even if we feel discouraged ourselves. Or making something special to eat. Or husband and wife giving one another some free time for recreation and renewal. Maybe we can cheerfully do something we don't really enjoy doing, but which gives someone else pleasure. If we're alert to such opportunities, we'll always find enough.

William Barclay wrote, "It is just by such deeds of understanding, simple kindliness that we too can show that we are followers of Jesus Christ."

 Lord Jesus, you showed your glory by helping a young couple at their wedding. Enable us to love one another with such deeds of simple kindness.

Do some special act of kindness for the family member you think needs your help most today.

■ THE SOUND OF MUSIC

Eph. 5:18-20: "Speak to one another with the words of psalms, hymns, and sacred songs" (v. 19).

Music is God's greatest gift," said Martin Luther, and it is surely one of the greatest gifts we can give to our children. The Bible even connects music and "being filled with the Spirit."

Music can help set the tone for our family living. A constant barrage of background noise leaves nerves on edge and destroys conversation. On the other hands, music can create a pleasant atmosphere and foster spiritual growth.

Best of all is active participation in music. Blessed is the family that can sing hymns at the table or join together around the piano. Children who play instruments can have their part. Bedtime can be made more enjoyable with singing or by listening to a favorite record. There is often good music on radio and TV. In place of a material gift, we can attend concerts or other musical events—many of which are free. Public libraries are a good source of records and tapes.

Especially as they enter the teenage years, our children will be exposed to music that is second-rate or even harmful. The best way to offset that is to start early to give them a positive appreciation for good music.

 O life-giving Spirit, we thank you for the gift of music. Show us how we can use this gift to increase family harmony.

Plan right now a specific way to make music a vehicle for the Spirit in your home.

■ FAVORITE SON

Gen. 37:1-4: "Jacob loved Joseph more than all his other sons" (v. 3).

Some say it was a coat of many colors. Others say it was a coat with long sleeves. Either way, it was a sign of the father's favoritism, and, as a result, Joseph's brothers hated him.

We probably all realize that we should not have favorites among our children, and that we will cause problems among them if we do. Yet it is hard to deny our human feelings. Some children are naturally more lovable or more responsive to us than others. We may prefer the child who shares our special interests or our temperament. The sex of a child or the order of birth may influence our feelings. We may not *feel* the same about each child.

But love is not just a matter of feelings. It is also a matter of the will. Despite our feelings, we can choose to treat our children fairly. This does not mean that we will treat them all *alike;* each child needs different treatment. It won't help to love our "favorite" child less; rather, we want to love the others more. The important thing is to give each child what he or she needs. In this way we follow God, who loves all his children, and, for this reason, gives to each one the special care that person needs.

 Lord, we thank you for loving each one of us in a special way. In the same way, enable us to love each one of our children.

Discuss whether you have a favorite child. Is this causing a problem in the family? If so, what can you do about it?

■ RIPPLES OF LOVE

Isa. 58:1-12: "If you give food to the hungry and satisfy those who are in need, then the darkness around you will turn to the brightness of noon" (v. 10).

Charity begins at home" is an old motto, which, like so many others, contains a profound truth. We do have a special call to love those nearest to us. Love should *begin* at home, but it should not *end* there. The family should not be the *exclusive* focus of our love.

The missionary-doctor Albert Schweitzer wrote: "It's not enough to say, 'I'm earning enough to love and to support my family. I do my work well. I'm a good father. I'm a good husband.' That's all very well. *But you must do something more.* Seek always to do some good, somewhere. Every man has to seek in his own way to make his self more noble and to realize his own true worth. You must give some time to your fellowman. Even if it's a little thing, do something for those who have need of help, something for which you get no pay but the privilege of doing it. For remember, you don't live in a world all your own. *Your brothers are here too.*"

As we receive God's love, we can share it—first with our family, then our neighborhood, our community, our country, the world. Then, like a pebble thrown into a pond, ripples of love will spread out from our home to all the world.

 Father, we thank you for your love for us. Lead us to share this love in our family, and then to all your children everywhere.

Discuss with your children how you can share God's love with needy people.

■ AT HOME AND AWAY

Deut. 6:1-9: "Repeat them when you are at home and when you are away, when you are resting and when you are working" (v. 7).

In these verses we have God's own plan for religious education.

It is centered, not in the church, but in the home.

It is based on our response to God's love. God had given Israel a land and his laws. Now he invites them to "love the Lord your God with all your heart, with all your soul, with all your strength."

It is informal. Parents are encouraged to remember God's commands and to teach them to their children, repeating them "at home and when you are away, when you are resting and when you are working."

It may involve visible reminders of the Word of God. The people of Israel were to tie Scripture verses on their arms, wear them on their foreheads, write them on their doorposts and on their gates.

Although we don't follow all these customs literally, we can follow their spirit. We can make our homes centers of religious education, responding to God's love for us. In addition to formal devotional times, we can talk of our spiritual beliefs in a natural way as we go about our daily life. We can display visible reminders of God's Word in the form of pictures, plaques, and posters.

If we are faithful in teaching and obeying God's Word, we have his promise: "then all will go well with you."

Lord, help us to share your Word with our children in the midst of our daily life together.

Place some visible reminder of God's Word in your home.

■ WE ARE NOT ALONE

1 Cor. 3:5-9: "I planted the seed, Apollos watered the plant, but it was God who made the plant grow" (v. 6).

An old proverb says, "God has no grandchildren." He has only sons and daughters. We are to pass on the Christian heritage, but each new generation must appropriate that heritage for itself.

We cannot believe for our children, and we cannot force them to believe. Faith is a gift of the Holy Spirit. We can only plant the seeds by our teaching and by the silent witness of our lives. Beyond that we trust in God.

We are not in this work by ourselves. As parents we may be the first to plant the seed. But God will send others to "water," to sow additional seeds, to prune and nourish the young plants: teachers, pastors, friends, relatives. He himself promises to make the plant grow.

There is great comfort in this picture: Paul planting, Apollos watering, God making the plants grow. It gives us a reasonable perspective on our own responsibility, a humble estimate of our own role, and it directs us to God himself: "The one who plants and the one who waters really do not matter. It is God who matters, because he makes the plant grow."

 Help us, O Lord, to plant good seeds in the lives of our children, and then trust that you will make them grow.

Who are the "Apollos" people in the lives of your children? How can you show your appreciation of them?

■ WHY, LORD?

John 9:1-7: "He is blind so that God's power might be seen at work in him" (v. 3).

Some friends gave birth to a child so severely retarded that he had to be institutionalized. The mother said that the cruelest words well-meaning people said to her were: "It must be God's will."

When a handicapped child is born or tragedy strikes a family, the old question quickly surfaces: "Why, Lord?" The disciples asked this question when they saw the blind man. Jesus made it clear—such difficulties are not to be thought of as God's punishment.

How then should we think of such evils? The Christian faith gives us no clear answer to the riddle of human suffering, and we probably will never unravel its mystery. The Bible does acknowledge that suffering is an integral part of the fallen world in which we live, and it directs us to our source of help, as Jesus did when he said, "He is blind so that *God's power* might be seen in him."

Through his power God either heals or he strengthens us to face the suffering. We can be reassured by the words of E. Stanley Jones: "There is no pain, no suffering, no frustration, no disappointment that cannot be cured or taken up and used for higher ends. In either case you have a way out. You are relieved of it or enriched by it."

O loving Lord, we know that your will for us is always good. We pray for your power to cope with all the problems we face.

Can you think of someone who is facing a difficult situation with courage and wisdom? What seems to be his or her secret?

■ THE NEED FOR HEROES

Heb. 12:1-2: "We have this large crowd of witnesses . . ." (v. 1).

In Hebrews, chapter 11, the writer gives us a catalog of some of the great heroes and heroines of the Bible: Abel, Enoch, Noah, Abraham, Moses, Rahab. Their faith is to inspire us to "rid ourselves of everything that gets in the way, and . . . run with determination the race that lies before us." We all need heroes and heroines to inspire us and to serve as models.

Children love heroes too, but our society may hold up to them the dubious celebrities of the entertainment or sports world. In place of the TV killer or racing car driver or tinselly actress, we can acquaint our children with men and women who are living out the values we associate with the Christian faith.

One way to do this is by reading to the children: first Bible stories of great people of faith, then biographies of some great Christian leaders of history. In our own day, too, there are men and women whose courage or compassion will inspire our children. By careful selection we can find some TV programs or movies that present people who make worthy heroes and heroines.

People like this can give us and our children a clearer vision of what we want to be and what we can become by the grace of God.

Heavenly Father, we thank you for the examples of the great men and women of faith who have gone before us. From them may we and our children learn what it means to be your people.

Identify your heroes and heroines. How can you hold them up before your children?

■ ALL ADOPTED CHILDREN

Gal. 4:4-7: ". . . that we might receive the adoption of sons" (v. 5 KJV).

It was an exciting moment when we entered the judge's chambers to complete the adoption of our son Paul. The judge asked a few preliminary questions, then said, "Do you realize that adoption is more permanent than marriage?"

We were stunned for a moment, because we had always thought of our marriage as a permanent commitment. But we realized then that before the law a marriage can be dissolved, while an adoption cannot. So Paul, as an adopted son, came into all the love and privileges of sonship.

The Bible tells us that we are all adopted children. God sent his Son to redeem us so that we could become members of God's family. Jesus obeyed God's law for us, so we can stand before God, not as obedient slaves, but as grateful children. God has chosen us, and his love will not let us go.

St. Augustine wrote, "Even when I turn to run from God, I hear his footsteps behind me." His love follows us and will not give up on us. We will always remain God's adopted children.

Heavenly Father, we thank you that you have chosen us and adopted us as your children. We are grateful, and we trust in your love, which will hold us forever.

Can you recall a time when you turned from God, yet he continued to demonstrate his loving concern for you?

■ LET GOD BE GOD

Matt. 10:34-39: "Whoever loves his son or daughter more than me is not fit to be my disciple" (v. 37).

God wants us to have our priorities straight, to know what belongs at the center of our life and what is on the periphery. Here, whether we like it or not, God makes the absolute claim: we must let God be God.

What does it mean to have a god? Martin Luther answers: "A god is that to which we look for all good and in which we find refuge in every time of need. . . . That to which your heart clings and entrusts itself is really your God."

God wants first place, not second. Everything which takes first place in our lives, besides God, is an idol. Even family can be an idol. Perhaps we know people whose entire lives revolve around their children; they have no other interests, no other goals. They may think they're doing a good thing, but that is too great a burden to place on a family. A family is not made to carry the weight which only God can carry.

The love of Jesus for us enables us to give our first love to God. We are then free to love and serve our family without demanding that they give what only God can give—ultimate security and meaning and love.

O Lord, we thank you that you are God, the center of all our lives and dreams. Help us give first place in our hearts to you.

Discuss whether there are any ways in which you expect from your family that which only God can give.

89

■ GOD'S DISCIPLINE

Prov. 3:11-18:   "Son, when the Lord corrects you, pay close attention and take it as a warning" (v. 11).

Because our heavenly Father loves us, he disciplines us. Perhaps his most common way is by using "logical consequences." That is, God disciplines us by letting us experience the results of our wrong actions. If we eat too much or drink too much, God may let us become sick. If we treat other people shabbily, we may know the loss of friendship. If we are careless about money, he may let us experience financial problems. This does not mean that every bad thing that happens to us is a sign that we are doing something wrong, but these reverses can encourage us to examine honestly some area of our life.

When we do experience these unhappy results, it is not because God is angry with us or trying to "get even." But he may be teaching us, showing us where our misguided actions will lead.

We know that we discipline our children because we care about them, and we hope that some day they will appreciate our discipline. So we should not despise the Lord's discipline of us, but thank him for giving us the awareness of our errors and the strength to overcome them.

 Lord, we thank you that you care enough about us to teach us your will. Help us to listen and learn, and give us strength to follow you.

Share a time when God's discipline was beneficial to you.

90

■ GOD LOOKS AT THE HEART

1 Sam. 16:1-13: "Man looks at the outward appearance, but I look at the heart" (v. 7).

God sent the prophet Samuel to anoint a new king, one to replace faithless Saul. The prophet came to Bethlehem to the home of the shepherd Jesse. One by one the sons of Jesse appeared before Samuel—tall, strong, handsome young men. And one by one Samuel rejected them. Finally he chose the least likely candidate, the youngest son, who would become the mighty King David. Samuel's explanation was simple, "Man looks at the outward appearance, but [God looks] at the heart."

We too may fall into the trap of judging our children by outward appearances—whether they are pretty or intelligent or athletic. It's easy in our society to fall into a "marketplace orientation" even toward our own children, judging them—or ourselves—by the traits that "sell" in our culture.

If we do that, we may miss some of the qualities God values—perhaps the ability to say a kind word, the gentle sympathy for things that hurt, the wide-eyed wonder over the intricacies of God's creation.

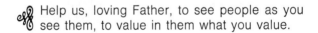 Help us, loving Father, to see people as you see them, to value in them what you value.

Can you recognize in your children the special qualities of the heart?

■ THE SEARCH FOR GREATNESS

Matt. 20:20-28: "If one of you wants to be great, he must be the servant of the rest" (v. 26).

A new book on childrearing, *How to Raise Your Child to Be a Winner,* offers advice on giving your child a head start in our competitive world.

It's natural for us to want our children to be successful, to be great. Jesus' definition of greatness, however, is the opposite of the world's. According to him, the great one is the one who serves.

It's as if God says to us, "It's all right for you to want to be first, to be a winner. But I want you to be first in love, first in generosity, first in service."

We need to remember that in the models we hold up to our children. Do we hold up only the successful businessman, the star athlete, the public official? Or do we remember to praise the humble examples of service: the teacher who goes the extra mile, the neighbor who is always quick to help, the relative who is kind in many small ways? We also need to remember to praise our children when they perform acts of kindness and consideration.

In our own family life we can demonstrate what it means to serve one another—and to serve our children. In so doing we follow Jesus, who washed his disciples' feet, and who came, not to be served, but to serve.

O Spirit of love, convince us that true greatness lies, not in dominating, but in serving.

How can you teach your children the greatness of serving?

■ CAUGHT, NOT TAUGHT

2 Tim. 1:3-7: "I remember the sincere faith you have, the kind of faith that your grandmother Lois and your mother Eunice also had" (v. 5).

Lois and Eunice are remembered in the Bible as the faithful grandmother and mother of Timothy, the young man who became Paul's most valued co-worker. Paul considered Timothy to be like his own son.

One of the reasons Timothy was so valued by Paul was because of his faith. Timothy had grown up in an atmosphere of faith, and through that experience God had given him faith.

Someone has said that faith is *caught, not taught.* Although we have a responsibility to teach the Christian faith, faith is transmitted more by our lives. The old principle "Do as I say, not as I do" just won't work. We have to do more than just talk about the faith; in fact, our children may well be "turned off" by our lecturing, especially if our lives do not match it.

But children will learn from our example—whether we like it or not! Our children will "catch" our faith as they see us making decisions, helping others, forgiving one another. They will "catch" our faith as we pray with them, sing with them, worship with them.

The more we can bring our own lives into harmony with our words, the more likely we are to pass on our faith to our children.

Lord, grant that our lives may be consistent with the faith we proclaim.

In what ways are you trying to pass on the faith to your children?

■ FORGIVENESS AND TRANSFORMATION

1 John 1:5-10: "He will forgive us our sins and purify us from all our wrongdoing" (v. 9).

With all the emphasis on the effects of the early years on children, we can become almost paranoid about making mistakes, afraid we will do permanent damage. We can become so concerned about this that we no longer act naturally. Our very desire for perfection may prevent us from giving our children the love and warmth they need.

We may as well realize that we will make mistakes. We will make wrong decisions. There will be times when patience runs out and we respond with anger, sarcasm, or selfishness. John said, "If we say that we have no sin, we deceive ourselves, and there is no truth in us."

But John also says if we confess our sins, God will forgive us and purify us. We don't have to be perfect parents. We can admit our faults to ourselves, to one another, to our children, and to God.

God will not only forgive us, but he can make up for our deficiencies. His power is at work in us to change us, to purify us from wrongdoing, and to transform us into better people and better parents.

With this assurance we can relax and enjoy our children more. We can live confidently, not as perfect parents, but as forgiven children of God.

 Lord, we are well aware of our mistakes and shortcomings as parents. We ask you to forgive us, purify us, transform us, and to make good come even from our mistakes.

Aloud—or silently—confess to God your sins as parents and ask God to change you.

■ THAT NAGGING HABIT

Prov. 15:1: "A gentle answer quiets anger, but a harsh one stirs it up."

If we could state three important rules for happy family living, they might be:
1. Don't nag.
2. Don't nag.
3. Don't nag.

Simple rules—but how hard to remember, and even harder to practice! It is so easy to fall into the habit of nagging the children or one another. Yet, with awareness and a full measure of God's grace, we can choose to ignore a particular problem or take some firm action to overcome it.

The dawdling child, for example, may be dragging her feet at getting ready in the morning just to seek attention or to prove she can control her own life. Nagging will only intensify the problem.

Instead we can let her experience the consequences of her actions—like missing the school bus. Or together we can work out a schedule for getting her ready on time. Books like Dreikurs' *Children: The Challenge* or Bruce Narramore's *Help, I'm a Parent!* can help us devise workable strategies. Nagging *can* be replaced by firm action and "a soft answer."

 Lord, make us aware of the simple habits that become a part of us. Free us to find better solutions to family problems.

Choose one area of family life where you are tempted to nag. What might be some constructive alternatives?

■ AND THEY BECOME ONE

Gen. 2:21-25: "That is why a man leaves his father
and mother and is united with his wife" (v. 24).

Since most of us have a relationship with our parents
and with our children, this Scripture verse has a
double edge.

In regard to our parents, it reminds us that our
relationship with our parents is meant to be temporary.
This knowledge can free us from the wrong kind of
emotional ties with a parent so that we can transfer
our affection to our spouse. It can also help us make
our own decisions, as a family, free from outside
pressure.

In regard to our own children, this verse can remind
us that there comes a time when we let go, when we
release them to new relationships.

This verse also reminds us to take good care of our
marriage. So many marriages collapse when the
children "leave the nest." Perhaps the father has been
too busy with his career, or the mother with the
children, to keep the marriage relationship healthy.

Remember that your marriage relationship will exist
when the children are gone. Build that close
relationship of "one flesh"—not just in sexual union,
but in a deep sharing of all of life.

Help us, Lord, to remember that our marriage
is more permanent than our parenting.

**This week do something special to strengthen your
marriage.**

■ SEVENTY TIMES SEVEN

Eph. 4:31-32: "Forgive one another, as God has forgiven you through Christ" (v. 32).

There are no perfect families, nor are there families without problems," writes Kenneth Chafin. "The difference between the healthy and the destructive family is not the absence of problems but how those problems are seen and dealt with."

One of the most important ways of dealing with the problems and conflicts that will always be there in our families is through forgiveness. Forgiveness is powerful enough to get rid of all "bitterness, passion, and anger." It is the answer to "shouting, or insults [or] hateful feelings."

Where can we find the motivation to forgive our children and one another? Paul tells us it is in the assurance that God has forgiven us through Christ. As forgiven sinners, we are free and bound to forgive others.

Peter once said, "How often must I forgive my brother when he sins against me?" Jesus answered, "Seventy times seven." Mother Teresa of Calcutta wrote, "We must make our homes centers of compassion and forgive endlessly."

 Forgiving God, we thank you for the grace and mercy you have shown us. May it move us to forgive our children and one another.

How can you best express forgiveness to one another?

■ GOD GIVES THE VICTORY

Rom. 7:14-25: "I don't do the good I want to do; instead, I do the evil that I do not want to do" (v. 19).

Sometimes we really don't know what to do as parents. We need God's guidance, and he has promised it.

But in many situations, we know what we should do or should not do. We know we should spend more time with the children, we know we should be more patient, we know we should do less fault-finding. Our problem is, how do we do it? Where do we get the power to do what we know we should do, and, indeed, what we want to do?

There's some comfort in knowing this is a universal Christian experience. Even Paul, counted the greatest of the apostles, felt the agonizing gap between his ideals and his performance. He cried out, "Who will rescue me from this body that is taking me to death?" Then he answered his own question: "Thanks be to God, who does this through our Lord Jesus Christ!"

There is no panacea, no "try this, and all your troubles will be over." We've learned to be suspicious of all such instant solutions. But we know that as we turn to God for help, he does give us victory—not always immediately or perfectly, but he does help. Always. He forgives, restores, strengthens, and empowers us.

 Lord of mercy and power, forgive us where we fall short, and give us victory where we most need it.

What is your greatest weakness as a parent? Right now ask God to give you victory there.

■ DISCOVER THE UNIQUENESS

Col. 1:24-29: ". . . to bring each one into God's presence as a mature individual in union with Christ" (v. 28).

We talked with someone recently who told about what he was doing to "mold" his children. That terminology bothered us. It suggested that children are lifeless clay, subject to our shaping according to our own design.

Paul's picture of Christian nurturing is different. It shows the Christian leader or parent as one who will "preach Christ," "warn," "teach," "toil and struggle." The goal is "to bring each one into God's presence as a mature individual." Paul's conviction is based on his belief in God's "rich and glorious secret," that Christ is in each one of us in a unique way.

That means our goal is not to *mold* our children, but to *discover* the unique expression of Christ within them. That leaves us free to accept them, even if they turn out different from us in some significant ways. Then we can help each one become his or her own best self, bringing each one "into God's presence as a mature individual in union with Christ."

Lord, we thank you for your great secret: that Christ lives in each one of us. Help us to respect and nurture the unique individuality of each child and each parent.

What are the distinctive marks of individuality in each child? How can you nurture these?

■ MENTAL DIET

Phil. 4:4-9: "Fill your minds with those things that are good and that deserve praise" (v. 8).

Junk food? We probably don't allow our children to eat a regular diet of it. We know enough about nutrition to realize that what they eat will make a big difference in their health and their well-being.

We're concerned too about the mental and spiritual diet of our children. How can we keep them away from other children who seem to be a bad influence? How can we prevent them from watching harmful TV programs? How can we stop them from wasting time on too many comic books?

While questions like these are necessary, they come at the problem only from the negative side. We may be better off approaching it positively, concentrating on discovering good activities, encouraging healthy relationships, watching together some worthwhile TV programs, listening to good music, reading aloud.

The other influences will still be there, but as we fill our children's lives with good, they will be less attracted to the bad.

This was Paul's approach too. He encouraged us to fill our minds with those things that are "true, noble, right, pure, lovely, and honorable."

 Lord, show us how we can fill our lives with good.

What's the mental diet of your family like? Find one new way in which you could build in more positive riches this week.

■ VALUABLE PEOPLE

Isa. 43:1-7: "I have called you by name—you are mine" (v. 1).

Fred Rogers, seen by millions of children each day as Mister Rogers, says the message he wants to get across on his television show is this: "There is just one person in the whole world like you. And people can like you just the way you are."

This is the message we want to get across to our children too. They are worthwhile and valuable people just because they are; they don't have to earn their sense of worth, and no one can take it from them.

We sometimes forget how often children need this message. Particularly in the early years of adolescence, children feel bad about themselves much of the time. This bad feeling may mask itself in anger or hostility. They need to hear over and over—in words and actions—that they are valuable and loved people who have eternal worth.

This sense of self-worth is rooted in God, based on God's declaration about each of us: "I have called you by name—you are mine."

We parents need this message too. We need to tell ourselves and one another that we have eternal value—because we belong to God.

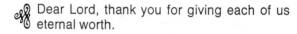 Dear Lord, thank you for giving each of us eternal worth.

Do something today to show all the members of your family they are valuable people.

■ GOD'S WORK

2 Cor. 4:1-12: "God in his mercy has given us this work to do, and so we do not become discouraged" (v. 1).

What a great encouragement there is in these words! It is God who has made us parents, giving us the gift and the responsibility of children. This knowledge can keep us from wallowing in the discouragement which overtakes us from time to time.

Perhaps it is young mothers at home who are especially vulnerable to this feeling of discouragement. Having only preschoolers for company all day is not easy. The endless round of cleaning and cooking and laundry can become boring and seem meaningless. Compounding the problem today is that society seems to put a higher value on the woman with a career than on the mother who stays home.

Maybe the words of Thomas Merton can help us regain our perspective: "The requirements of a work to be done can be understood as the will of God. If I am supposed to hoe a garden or make a table, then I will be obeying God if I am true to the task I am performing. To do the work carefully and well, with love and respect for the nature of my task and with due attention to its purpose, is to unite myself to God's will in my work. In this way I become his instrument. He works through me."

St. Paul said: "Nothing you do in the Lord's service is ever useless" (1 Cor. 15:58).

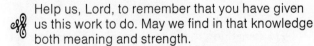

Help us, Lord, to remember that you have given us this work to do. May we find in that knowledge both meaning and strength.

Choose a quote from this reading and place it where you can see it often during the day.

■ BEING PRESENT TO ONE ANOTHER

Psalm 16: "Your presence fills me with joy" (v. 11).

A friend once said about a teacher he admired: "When you're with him, he's always *all there.*" Once I was with an evangelist who spoke at a youth rally to hundreds of teenagers. After the meeting dozens of the young people lined up to talk with him. Even though he had a plane to catch, he ignored the crowd and spoke to each person as if that were the only person in the world.

It is a small thing we can do for one another—but how important—just being *all there!* It's not easy when our minds are filled with responsibilities and tasks of the day, but it's a discipline that can be learned with practice. And it is a wonderful way of expressing our love for the person we are with.

In our busy lives we may not always be able to be with our children as much as we would like. But the *quantity* of time we spend is not as important as the *quality.* We can concentrate on making the time we do spend with them good time.

Mother Teresa says of the dying poor to whom she ministers in India: "Every person is Christ for me, and since there is only one Jesus, that person is the one person in the world at that moment."

 Heavenly Father, we thank you that you are always present with us. Enable us to be truly present to one another.

The next time you're with one of your children, just try to be *all there.*

■ LET GOD TAKE OVER

1 Peter 5:7: "Leave all your worries with him, because he cares for you."

When family problems weigh us down, we can end up lying awake at night, turning them over and over in our minds, fretting and fussing until sleep becomes impossible. There is a better way. A friend said he learned to pray, "Lord, I've been taking care of this world all day; now you can take over."

This is the attitude which God invites when he encourages us to "leave all our worries with him." This is not an irresponsible stance, as if we did not care what happened, but a realistic assessment of our own limitations and a heartfelt trust in God's willingness to help.

This verse instructs us to *leave* all our worries with God. This is an important point, for too often we give our problems to God, but then we hang on to them, so they bounce back like a ball on a rubber band.

By a regular discipline of our minds we can practice the attitude of Leslie Weatherhead: "You cannot get tomorrow's strength until tomorrow. Why then try to carry tomorrow's burden today? One day's worries are quite enough for one day."

 Lord, we thank you that we can bring all our troubles to you in prayer. Help us to leave them there.

Memorize these words and use them when you're tempted to worry: "God has brought me through today; he will bring me through tomorrow."

104

■ LEARNING BY IMITATION

Phil. 3:17-21: "Keep on imitating me" (v. 17).

We were once fortunate enough to visit the Louvre, one of the great art museums of the world. There we saw art students from many countries copying the great masterpieces. They were learning to paint by imitating the masters.

Our children, too, will learn far more from our actions than from our words. They *will* learn from our example—whether we want them to or not.

God himself used this method. After speaking through his prophets, he finally sent his Son to show what a human life could be.

Does this place an intolerable burden on us as parents? It would if it meant we had to be perfect. But we can let our children imitate us also in this— that we do not claim to be perfect, that we confess our sins to God and to one another, and that we ask for forgiveness.

A friend said, "When we make mistakes and get irritated and frustrated, we remember that our children would be totally unprepared to live in an imperfect world if they lived in a perfect home." That realistic wisdom is reassuring. Let us then trust that our children will see beyond our surface faults to the inner spirit that motivates us.

 Heavenly Father, give us the power to imitate Christ. May our lives be consistent with our words.

Can you identify ways—for good or bad—in which your children imitate you?

■ LIFE IS HARD

John 16:25-33: "The world will make you suffer. But be brave! I have defeated the world!" (v. 33).

A boy came home from school, threw his books on the kitchen table, and exclaimed, "Mom, if you think your life is hard, you ought to be out on the playground at recess!"

Enmeshed in our own problems, we sometimes forget that children's problems are just as big to them as ours are to us. Since time has a way of mellowing memories, we may forget the pain children often feel, their bewilderment, their fears, their suffering from other children's cruelty.

In many cases we can't solve these problems for our children—nor would that necessarily be best for them. We can, of course, avoid ridiculing them or minimizing their problems. We can encourage them to talk things out. We can pray for them and teach them to draw on the ever-present help of God.

Perhaps the problems that look so overwhelming to us also take on a different perspective in the eyes of our heavenly Father. His power is always greater than our problems. "To him who by means of his power working in us is able to do so much more than we can ever ask for, or even think of: to God be the glory in the church and in Christ Jesus for all time, forever and ever! Amen" (Eph. 3:20-21).

Lord, teach us to see our children's problems through their eyes—and also through yours.

Can you identify the chief problem each of your children faces? Take time now to pray about that.

■ WHY WORRY?

Matt. 6:25-34:   ". . . why do you worry . . . ?"
(v. 28 NIV)

When we brought our first baby home from the hospital, we were afraid to hold her and handle her, as if she might break. With the first child we responded to every cry, every minor hurt. At the first sign of misbehavior we were quick to correct. We kept a rigid schedule. We were afraid that the slightest mistake would cause permanent damage.

All the parents we know agree that they were far more strict and more worried about their first child. By the time the younger ones come along, you are too busy—or too *tired*—to fuss that much. You've learned from experience that children are not so breakable, that problems have a way of working out, and that God really does take care of you. So maybe you relax a bit and enjoy your children more. And somehow the younger ones turn out just as well—or maybe even better—without all our worrying.

It's a great lesson to learn, and to keep on learning. We try our best as parents, but at the same time we relax, knowing we are buoyed up by God's grace, that God knows our needs, that his loving help is always near.

O faithful Lord, when we become worried, help us to lean back on your grace.

What are your greatest worries about family life right now? Take a few moments to pray about this and to reassure one another of God's help.

■ PRAYING FOR ONE ANOTHER

2 Thess. 3:1-5: "Finally, our brothers, pray for us" (v. 1).

There is great power in intercessory prayer. Such prayer does not change God, but it releases his power to work in the life of another. Praying for someone can change us as well, deepening our love, dissolving our resentment, and increasing our commitment to be involved in God's helping action.

No one has said it better than Dietrich Bonhoeffer: "A Christian fellowship lives and exists by the intercession of its members for one another, or it collapses. I can no longer condemn or hate a brother for whom I pray, no matter how much trouble he causes me. His face . . . is transformed in intercession into the countenance of a brother for whom Christ died, the face of a forgiven sinner. This is a happy discovery. . . . There is no dislike, no personal tension, no estrangement that cannot be overcome by intercession. . . . Intercessory prayer is the purifying bath into which the individual and the fellowship must enter every day. The struggle we undergo with our brother in intercession may be a hard one, but that struggle has the promise that it will gain its goal."

Blessed is that family whose members have learned to pray for one another!

Thank you for the gift of prayer. Move us to be faithful to this gift.

Let those family members who are old enough agree to pray for one another daily.

BIBLE READINGS SERIES

Bible Readings for Women
    Lyn Klug
Bible Readings for Men
    Steve Swanson
Bible Readings for Parents
    Ron and Lyn Klug
Bible Readings for Couples
    Margaret and Erling Wold
Bible Readings for Singles
    Ruth Stenerson
Bible Readings for Families
    Mildred and Luverne Tengbom
Bible Readings for Teenagers
    Charles S. Mueller
Bible Readings for Mothers
    Mildred Tengbom
Bible Readings for Teachers
    Ruth Stenerson
Bible Readings for Students
    Ruth Stenerson
Bible Readings for the Retired
    Leslie F. Brandt
Bible Readings for Church Workers
    Harry N. Huxhold
Bible Readings for Office Workers
    Lou Ann Good
Bible Readings for Growing Christians
    Kevin E. Ruffcorn
Bible Readings for Caregivers
    Betty Groth Syverson
Bible Readings for Troubled Times
    Leslie F. Brandt
Bible Readings for Farm Living
    Frederick Baltz
Bible Readings on Prayer
    Ron Klug
Bible Readings on Hope
    Roger C. Palms
Bible Readings on God's Creation
    Denise J. Williamson